Rick Steves

POCKET
VENICE

Rick Steves & Gene Openshaw

Contents

Introduction

Venice is a world apart. Built on a hundred islands, its exotic-looking palaces are laced together by graceful bridges over sun-speckled canals. Romantics revel in the city's atmosphere of elegant decay. And first-time visitors are often stirred deeply, waking from their ordinary lives to a fantasy world unlike anything they've ever seen.

Those are strong reactions, considering that Venice today, frankly, can also be an overcrowded tourist trap. But Venice offers so much. By day, it's a city of art-filled museums, trendy shops, and narrow alleyways. At night, when the hordes of day-trippers have gone, another Venice appears. Glide in a gondola through quiet canals. Dance across a floodlit square. Don a Carnevale mask—or just a fresh shirt—and become someone else for a night.

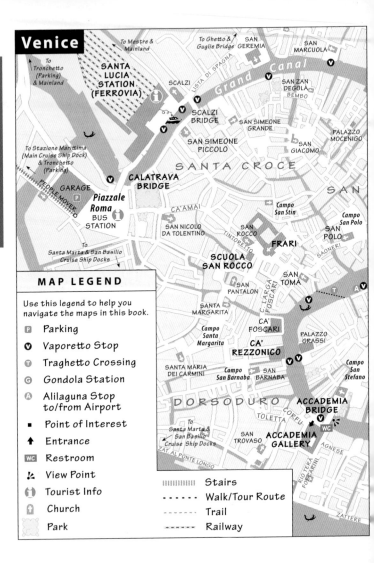

Venice

To Mestre & Mainland
To Ghetto & Guglie Bridge

SAN GEREMIA
SAN MARCUOLA

To Tronchetto (Parking) & Mainland

SANTA LUCIA STATION (FERROVIA)

SCALZI

LISTA DI SPAGNA

Grand Canal

SAN ZAN DEGOLÀ
BEMBO

SCALZI BRIDGE

SAN SIMEONE GRANDE

PALAZZO MOCENIGO

To Stazione Marittima (Main Cruise Ship Dock) & Tronchetto (Parking)

SAN SIMEONE PICCOLO

SAN GIACOMO

SANTA CROCE

SAN

GARAGE
PEOPLE MOVER
P

CALATRAVA BRIDGE

Piazzale Roma
BUS STATION

CA'AMAI

Campo San Stin

Campo San Polo

SAN POLO

To Santa Marta & San Basilio Cruise Ship Docks

SAN NICOLO DA TOLENTINO

SAN ROCCO

TINTORETTO

FRARI

SAONERI

SCUOLA SAN ROCCO

SAN TOMA

MAP LEGEND

SAN PANTALON

C. LARGA FOSCARI

Use this legend to help you navigate the maps in this book.

SANTA MARGARITA

T

A

P	Parking
V	Vaporetto Stop
T	Traghetto Crossing
G	Gondola Station
A	Alilaguna Stop to/from Airport
■	Point of Interest
✦	Entrance
WC	Restroom
⌁	View Point
⛟	Tourist Info
⛪	Church
	Park

Campo Santa Margarita

CA' FOSCARI

CA' REZZONICO

PALAZZO GRASSI

Campo San Stefano

SANTA MARIA DEI CARMINI

Campo San Barnaba

SAN BARNABA

DORSODURO

ACCADEMIA BRIDGE

CORFU

TOLETTA

WC

To Santa Marta & San Basilio Cruise Ship Docks

SAN TROVASO

ACCADEMIA GALLERY

AGNESE

ZAT. AL PONTE LONGO

RIO TERA FOSCARINI

ZATTERE

▒▒▒▒	Stairs
- - - -	Walk/Tour Route
- - - -	Trail
- - - -	Railway

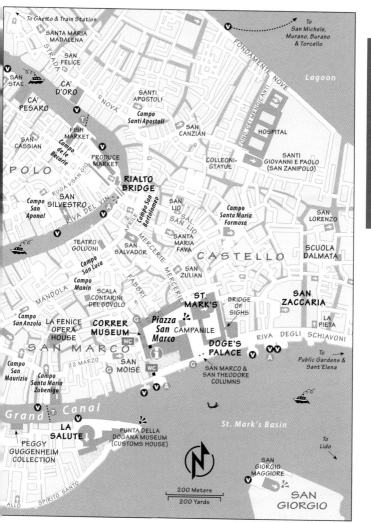

To Ghetto & Train Station

SANTA MARIA MADALENA

SAN FELICE

To San Michele, Murano, Burano & Torcello

FONDAMENTE NOVE

Lagoon

SAN STAE

CA' D'ORO

CA' PESARO

SANTI APOSTOLI

Campo Santi Apostoli

SAN CANZIAN

HOSPITAL

SAN CASSIAN

FISH MARKET

Campo de le Becarie

PRODUCE MARKET

COLLEONI STATUE

SANTI GIOVANNI E PAOLO (SAN ZANIPOLO)

POLO

RIALTO BRIDGE

SAN SILVESTRO

Campo San Aponal

RUGA VSAN GIO

RIVA DEL VIN

Campo San Bartolomeo

SAN LIO

SAL LIO

Campo Santa Maria Formosa

SAN LORENZO

TEATRO GOLDONI

SAN SALVADOR

Campo San Luca

MERCERIE

SANTA MARIA FAVA

CASTELLO

SCUOLA DALMATA

Campo Manin

SAN ZULIAN

MANDOLA

SCALA CONTARINI DEL BOVOLO

FABRI

MERCERIE

ST. MARK'S

BRIDGE OF SIGHS

SAN ZACCARIA

Campo San Anzolo

LA FENICE OPERA HOUSE

CORRER MUSEUM

Piazza San Marco

CAMPANILE

DOGE'S PALACE

LA PIETA

SAN MARCO

22 MARZO

SAN MOISÈ

WC

RIVA DEGLI SCHIAVONI

To Public Gardens & Sant'Elena

Campo San Maurizio

Campo Santa Maria Zobenigo

SAN MARCO & SAN THEODORE COLUMNS

Grand Canal

LA SALUTE

PUNTA DELLA DOGANA MUSEUM (CUSTOMS HOUSE)

St. Mark's Basin

To Lido

PEGGY GUGGENHEIM COLLECTION

SPIRITO SANTO

ALLO

200 Meters

200 Yards

SAN GIORGIO MAGGIORE

SAN GIORGIO

Key to This Book

Sights are rated:

▲▲▲ **Don't miss**

▲▲ **Try hard to see**

▲ **Worthwhile if you can make it**

No rating **Worth knowing about**

Tourist information offices are abbreviated as **TI,** and bathrooms are WCs.

Like Europe, this book uses the **24-hour clock.** It's the same through 12:00 noon, then keeps going: 13:00 (1:00 p.m.), 14:00 (2:00 p.m.), and so on.

For **opening times,** if a sight is listed as "May-Oct daily 9:00-16:00," it should be open from 9 a.m. until 4 p.m. from the first day of May until the last day of October (but expect exceptions).

For **updates** to this book, visit www.ricksteves.com/update.

About This Book

With this book, I've selected only the best of Venice—admittedly, a tough call. The core of the book is eight self-guided tours that zero in on Venice's greatest sights and neighborhoods.

My Grand Canal Cruise, snaking through the heart of the historic core, introduces you to this moist metropolis. Then hit St. Mark's Square, with its one-of-a-kind basilica and Doge's Palace. I've included several neighborhood walks that take you to major sights (Rialto Bridge) and out-of-the-way places (Frari Church).

The rest of the book is a traveler's tool kit. You'll find plenty more about Venice's attractions, from shopping to nightlife to how to do a Venetian pub crawl. And there are helpful hints on saving money, avoiding crowds, getting around town, enjoying a great meal, and more.

Venice by Neighborhood

The island city of Venice (population under 55,000) is shaped like a fish. Its major thoroughfares are canals. The Grand Canal winds through the middle of the fish, starting at the mouth where all the people and food enter, passing under the Rialto Bridge, and ending at St. Mark's Square (Piazza San Marco). Park your 21st-century perspective at the mouth and let Venice swallow you whole.

The easiest way to navigate is by landmarks. Many street corners have a sign pointing you to (per) the nearest major landmark. St. Mark's Square (San Marco) and Rialto Bridge are the center of the tourist action. Other major landmarks are Accademia Bridge (gateway to the charming Dorsoduro neighborhood), Ferrovia (train station), and Piazzale Roma (another transportation hub). I've organized this book—sights, hotels, and restaurants—around these major landmarks.

Officially, Venice is divided into six districts, called *sestieri* (see the map). Addresses generally list the district and house number (e.g., Cannaregio #221b), not the street. For more on the *sestieri* and addresses, see page 186. I find it easier to navigate by landmarks, not *sestieri*, addresses, or street names.

Venice is small. You can walk across it in an hour, and most sights are within 20 minutes of the Rialto Bridge or St. Mark's Square. Beyond the city's core lie several other interesting islands (Murano, Burano, Torcello, Lido) accessible only by boat.

Planning Your Time

Plan your sightseeing carefully to avoid lines and work around closed

INTRODUCTION

▲▲▲ **St. Mark's Square** Venice's grand main square. See page 29.

▲▲▲ **St. Mark's Basilica** Cathedral with mosaics, saint's bones, treasury, museum, and viewpoint of square. **Hours:** Mon-Sat 9:45-17:00, Sun 14:00-17:00 (Sun until 16:00 Nov-Easter). See page 43.

▲▲▲ **Doge's Palace** Art-splashed palace of former rulers, with prison accessible through Bridge of Sighs. **Hours:** Daily 8:30-19:00, Nov-March until 17:30. See page 65.

▲▲▲ **Rialto Bridge** Distinctive bridge spanning the Grand Canal, with a market nearby. **Hours:** Souvenir stalls open daily, produce market closed Sun, fish market closed Sun-Mon. See page 139.

▲▲ **Correr Museum** Venetian history and art. **Hours:** Daily 10:00-19:00, Nov-March until 17:00. See page 127.

▲▲ **Accademia** Venice's top art museum. **Hours:** Mon 8:15-14:00, Tue-Sun until 19:15. See page 132.

▲▲ **Peggy Guggenheim Collection** Popular display of 20th-century art. **Hours:** Wed-Mon 10:00-18:00, closed Tue. See page 134.

▲▲ **Frari Church** Franciscan church featuring Renaissance masters. **Hours:** Mon-Sat 9:00-18:00, Sun 13:00-18:00. See page 83.

▲▲ **Scuola San Rocco** "Tintoretto's Sistine Chapel." **Hours:** Daily 9:30-17:30. See page 139.

days. (See my sightseeing tips on page 192.) Venice is small enough that, even if you only had one day, you could see the biggies in a 12-hour sightseeing blitz. But let's assume you have at least three days.

Day 1: In the morning, take the slow vaporetto #1 down the Grand Canal from the train station/Piazzale Roma to San Marco. Ride to the top of the Campanile, and then take my self-guided St. Mark's Square Tour. Explore the Rialto market, grabbing lunch at the *cicchetti* bars nearby. Then spend the afternoon sightseeing the basilica, the Doge's Palace, and the Correr Museum. Around 19:00, have dinner (make a reservation). Afterward, enjoy the dueling orchestras with a drink on St. Mark's Square.

▲ **Campanile** Dramatic bell tower on St. Mark's Square with elevator to the top. **Hours:** Daily 8:30-21:00, Sept-mid-Oct until sunset, mid-Oct-April 9:30-17:30. See page 129.

▲ **Bridge of Sighs** Famous enclosed bridge, part of Doge's Palace, near St. Mark's Square. **Hours:** Always viewable. See page 126.

▲ **San Giorgio Maggiore** Island facing St. Mark's Square, featuring dreamy church and fine views back on Venice. **Hours:** Daily 9:00-19:00, Nov-March 8:30-18:00. See page 130.

▲ **La Salute Church** Striking church dedicated to the Virgin Mary. **Hours:** Daily 9:00-12:00 & 15:00-17:30. See page 136.

▲ **Ca' Rezzonico** Posh Grand Canal palazzo with 18th-century Venetian art. **Hours:** Wed-Mon 10:00-18:00, Nov-March until 17:00, closed Tue year-round. See page 137.

▲ **Punta della Dogana** Museum of contemporary art. **Hours:** Wed-Mon 10:00-19:00, closed Tue. See page 138.

Church of San Zaccaria Final resting place of St. Zechariah, plus a Bellini altarpiece and an eerie crypt. **Hours:** Mon-Sat 10:00-12:00 & 16:00-18:00, Sun 16:00-18:00. See page 118.

Day 2: Spend the morning shopping and exploring (consider my Rialto to Frari Church Walk) as you make your way to the Frari Church. See the Frari and head over to the Accademia/Dorsoduro area and have lunch. Spend the afternoon seeing the Dorsoduro's main artsy sights: Ca' Rezzonico, Accademia, and the Peggy Guggenheim Collection. Or take a nap. Around 18:00, do a pub crawl for dinner. Afterward, take a gondola ride (or, much cheaper, a moonlight vaporetto ride).

Day 3 and Beyond: Choose from among Venice's lesser sights: a trip to San Giorgio Maggiore, La Salute, modern art at the Punta della Dogana, or the area east of St. Mark's (Church of San Zaccaria,

Daily Reminder

Sunday: While anyone is welcome to worship, most churches are closed to sightseers on Sunday morning. They reopen in the afternoon: St. Mark's Basilica (14:00-17:00, until 16:00 Nov-Easter), Frari Church (13:00-18:00), and the Church of San Zaccaria (16:00-18:00). The Rialto open-air market consists mainly of souvenir stalls (fish and produce sections closed). It's a bad day for a pub crawl, as most pubs are closed.

Monday: All sights are open except the Rialto fish market, Ca' Pesaro, Palazzo Mocenigo Costume Museum, Lace Museum (on the island of Burano), and Torcello church museum (on the island of Torcello). The Accademia and Ca' d'Oro close at 14:00.

Tuesday: All sights are open except the Peggy Guggenheim Collection, Ca' Rezzonico (Museum of 18th-Century Venice), and Punta della Dogana.

Wednesday/Thursday/Friday: All sights are open.

Saturday: All sights are open except the Jewish Museum.

Notes: The Accademia is open earlier (daily at 8:15) and closes later (19:15 Tue-Sun) than most sights in Venice. Some sights close earlier off-season (such as the Correr Museum, Campanile bell tower, St. Mark's Basilica, and the Church of San Giorgio Maggiore). Modest dress is recommended at churches and required at St. Mark's Basilica—no bare shoulders, shorts, or short skirts.

Scuola Dalmata di San Giorgio). Budget time for just exploring, using my walks as a jumping-off point. In the evening, have dinner and catch a Vivaldi concert. With more time in Venice, you could visit the lagoon islands (Murano, Burano, and more), but these require at least a half-day.

Quick Tips: Avoid the midday crowds around St. Mark's as best you can. Take advantage of my free Venice 🎧 audio tours, covering the Grand Canal Cruise, St. Mark's Square, St. Mark's Basilica, and the Frari Church—see page 193 for details. A vaporetto pass and a Museum Pass may be worthwhile. Consider an afternoon nap to maximize energy for after dark. Stop often for gelato.

Finally, remember that Venice itself is its greatest sight. Make time to wander, shop, and simply be. When you cross a bridge, look both ways. You may be hit with a lovely view.

I hope you have a great trip! Traveling like a temporary local and taking advantage of the information here, you'll enjoy the absolute most out of every mile, minute, and dollar. I'm happy that you'll be visiting places I know and love, and meeting some of my favorite Italian people.

Happy travels! *Buon viaggio!*

Grand Canal Cruise

Canal Grande

Take a joyride and introduce yourself to Venice by boat. Cruise the Canal Grande all the way from the train station (Ferrovia) to St. Mark's Square.

If it's your first trip down the Grand Canal, you might want to stow this book and just take it all in—Venice is a barrage on the senses that hardly needs narration. On the other hand, these notes give the cruise meaning and help orient you to this great city.

I've organized this tour by boat stop. I'll point out what you can see from the current stop, and what to look forward to as you cruise to the next stop. Now, kick back and let Venice entertain you with its charms.

ORIENTATION

Length of This Tour: Allow 45 minutes.

Cost: €7.50 for a 75-minute vaporetto ticket, or covered by a transit pass—the best choice if you want to hop on and off (see page 189).

When to Go: Avoid the morning rush hour (8:00-10:00), when everyone is headed toward San Marco. In the uncrowded evening, sunset bathes the buildings in gold; after dark, chandeliers light up building interiors.

Getting There: This tour starts at the Ferrovia vaporetto stop (at Santa Lucia train station). It also works if you board upstream from Ferrovia at Piazzale Roma, a short walk over the Calatrava Bridge.

Catching Your Boat: This tour is designed to be done on the slow boat #1, which takes about 45 minutes. The express boat #2 travels the same route, but it skips some stops and takes 25 minutes, making it hard to sightsee. Also, some #2 boats terminate at Rialto; confirm that you're on a boat that goes all the way to San Marco.

Audio Tour: 🎧 If you download my free audio tour (see page 193), you won't even have to look at the book.

Stops to Consider: Consider hopping on and off along the way. Some interesting stops are: San Marcuola (Jewish Ghetto), Rialto Mercato (fish market and famous bridge), Ca' Rezzonico (Museum of 18th-Century Venice), Accademia (art museum and the nearby Peggy Guggenheim Collection), and La Salute (huge art-filled church).

Sightseeing Tips: Try to snag a seat in the bow (though not all boats have them). You're more likely to find an empty seat if you catch the vaporetto at Piazzale Roma. For views, the left side has a slight edge, with more sights and the best light late in the day.

Frankly, it's hard to sightsee while reading aboard a moving boat. Some readers do this cruise twice—once in either direction—to enjoy it all.

Starring: Palaces, markets, boats, bridges—Venice.

BACKGROUND

While you wait for your boat, here's some background on Venice's "Main Street."

At more than two miles long, nearly 150 feet wide, and nearly 15 feet deep, the Grand Canal is the city's largest canal, lined with its most impressive palaces. It's the remnant of a river that once spilled from the mainland into the Adriatic. The sediment it carried formed barrier islands that cut Venice off from the sea, forming a lagoon.

Venice was built on the marshy islands of the former delta, sitting on wood pilings driven nearly 15 feet into the clay (alder was the preferred wood). About 25 miles of canals drain the city, dumping like streams into the Grand Canal. Technically, Venice has only three canals: Grand, Giudecca, and Cannaregio. The 45 small waterways that dump into the Grand Canal are referred to as rivers (e.g., Rio Novo).

Venice is a city of palaces, dating from the days when the city was the world's richest. The most lavish palaces formed a grand architectural cancan along the Grand Canal. Once frescoed in reds and blues, with black-and-white borders and gold-leaf trim, they made Venice a city of dazzling color. This cruise is the only way to truly appreciate the palaces, approaching them at water level, where their main entrances were located. Today, strict laws prohibit any changes in these buildings, so while landowners gnash their teeth, we can enjoy Europe's best-preserved medieval/Renaissance city—slowly rotting.

Grand Canal

To Jewish Ghetto

SAN GEREMIA

PALAZZO CORRER CONTARINI

San Marcuola

SAN MARCUOLA

PAL. GRITTI

CASINÒ

PAL. VENDRAMIN CALERGI

LISTA DI SPAGNA

PALAZZO FLANGINI

Riva di Biasio

PAL. GIO-VANELLI

TURKISH EXCHANGE

SANTA LUCIA TRAIN STATION (FERROVIA)

SCALZI

PALAZZO CALBO-CROTTA

PAL. MARCELLO

SCALZI BRIDGE

PAL. GRITTI

PALAZZO DONÀ BALBI

SAN ZAN DEGOLÀ

PALAZZO CA' TRON

Ferrovia ❶

SANTA CROCE

TOUR BEGINS

SAN SIMEONE PICCOLO

CALATRAVA BRIDGE

GARAGE

P

PIAZZALE ROMA

SAN

PEOPLE MOVER
To Stazione Marittima (Main Cruise Ship Dock) & Tronchetto (Parking)

SAN POLO

FRARI

PALAZZO CAPPELLO-LAYARD

SCUOLA SAN ROCCO

SAN TOMÀ

PALAZZO BARBARIGO

PALAZZO GIUSTINIANI

Sant' Angelo ❾

PALAZZO BALBI

San Tomà ❿

PALAZZO MOCENIGO

FIRE STATION

CA' FOSCARI

PALAZZO VECCHIA

PALAZZO MORO LIN

PALAZZO GRASSI

PALAZZO GIUSTINIAN

CA' REZZONICO

Ca' Rezzonico ⓫

PALAZZO MALIPIERO-CAPPELLO

PALAZZO LOREDAN

PALAZZO FALIER

PALAZZO CONTARINI DEGLI SCRIGNI

Accademia

PALAZZO GIUSTINIAN LOLIN

PALAZZO QUERINI

⓬

PALAZZO BARBARO

ACCADEMIA BRIDGE & GALLERY

PALAZZO BARBARIGO

Grand

Vaporetto Stops

❶ Ferrovia
❷ Riva de Biasio
❸ San Marcuola
❹ San Stae
❺ Ca' d'Oro
❻ Rialto Mercato
❼ Rialto
❽ San Silvestro
❾ Sant'Angelo
❿ San Tomà
⓫ Ca' Rezzonico
⓬ Accademia
⓭ Santa Maria del Giglio
⓮ Salute
⓯ San Marco
⓰ San Zaccaria

PALAZZO
MARCELLO

PALAZZO MOLIN

PALAZZO ZULLAN

PALAZZO BARBARIGO

Fondamenta Nove

To
San Michele,
Murano,
Burano &
Torcello

FONDAMENTE NOVE

Lagoon

4 San Stae
**SAN
STAE**

PALAZZO
FONTANA

PAL.
DONA

PALAZZO
GIUSTI

'CA'
D'ORO'

PALAZZO
SAGREDO

**CA'
PESARO**

PAL.
FAVRETTO

PALAZZO
MICHIEL COLONNE

STRADA NOVA

PAL.
BRANDO-
LIN

5 Ca d'Oro

PALAZZO
VALMARANA

PALAZZO
CORNER
DELLA REGINA

**FISH
MARKET**

6

PALAZZO
CA' DA MOSTO

Rialto
Mercato

**PRODUCE
MARKET**

PALAZZO
CIVRAN

P O L O

CANNAREGIO

HOSPITAL

SANTI
GIOVANNI E PAOLO
(SAN ZANIPOLO)

**FONDACO DEI
TEDESCHI**
(FORMER GERMAN
EXCHANGE)

PALAZZO
PAPADOPOLI

**RIALTO
BRIDGE**

PALAZZO
BARZIZZA

7 Rialto

PALAZZO
DOLFIN-MANIN

SAL. S. LIO

S. MARIA
FORMOSA

PALAZZO
DONA

8 San
Silvestro

PALAZZO
BEMBO

MERCERIE

PALAZZO
BERNARDO

PALAZZO
GRIMANI

PALAZZO
FARSETTI-DANDOLO

C A S T E L L O

PALAZZO
BENZON

PAL.
CORNER-
CONTARINI

PALAZZO
CORNER-
SPINELLI

PALAZZO
MARTINENGO

FABBRI

MERCERIE

CLOCK
TOWER

**ST.
MARK'S
BASILICA**

SAN
ZACCARIA

CAMPANILE

**SAN
MARCO**

**DOGE'S
PALACE**

**BRIDGE
OF SIGHS**

S A N   M A R C O

CALLE LARGA
XXII MARZO

HARRY'S
AMERICAN
BAR

SAN MARCO &
SAN THEODORE
COLUMNS

TOUR ENDS

San Zaccaria

16

To
Lido

**GRITTI
PALACE
HOTEL**

CA'
GRANDE

Santa Maria
del Giglio

PALAZZO
FLANGINI

15

San Marco

A

**St. Mark's
Basin**

13

**PEGGY
GUGGEN.**

PAL.
GENOVESE

Salute

**14 LA
SALUTE
CHURCH**

**PUNTA DELLA
DOGANA MUSEUM
(CUSTOMS HOUSE)**

To
San Giorgio
Maggiore &
Giudecca

200 Meters

200 Yards

Many of the grand buildings are now vacant. Others harbor chandeliered elegance above mossy, empty (often flooded) ground floors.

THE TOUR BEGINS

❶ Ferrovia

The **Santa Lucia train station,** one of the few modern buildings in town, was built in 1954. It's been the gateway into Venice since 1860, when the first station was built. The "F.S." logo above the entry stands for "Ferrovie dello Stato," the Italian state railway system.

More than 20,000 people a day commute in from the mainland, making this the busiest part of Venice during rush hour. The **Calatrava Bridge** (see page 144), spanning the Grand Canal between the train station and Piazzale Roma upstream, was built in 2008 to alleviate some of the congestion.

❷ Riva de Biasio

Venice's main thoroughfare is busy with all kinds of **boats:** taxis, police boats, garbage boats, ambulances, construction cranes, and even brown-and-white UPS boats. Somehow they all manage to share the canal in relative peace.

About 25 yards past the Riva de Biasio stop, look left down the broad **Cannaregio Canal** to see what was the **Jewish Ghetto** (described on page 142). The twin, pale-pink, six-story "skyscrapers"—the tallest buildings you'll see at this end of the canal—are reminders of how densely populated the neighborhood was. Founded in 1516 near

Ferrovia, a.k.a. Santa Lucia train station

The Grand Canal, lined with grand buildings

a copper foundry (geto), this segregated community gave us our word "ghetto."

❸ San Marcuola

At this stop, facing a tiny square just ahead, stands the unfinished Church of San Marcuola, one of only five churches fronting the Grand Canal. Centuries ago, this canal was a commercial drag of expensive real estate in high demand by wealthy merchants. About 20 yards ahead on the right stands the stately gray **Turkish Exchange (Fondaco dei Turchi),** one of the oldest houses in Venice. Its horseshoe arches and roofline of triangles and dingle balls are reminders of its Byzantine heritage. Turkish traders in turbans docked here, unloaded their goods into the warehouse on the bottom story, and then went upstairs for a home-style meal and a place to sleep. Venice in the 1500s was very cosmopolitan, welcoming every religion and ethnicity, so long as they carried cash. (Today the building contains the city's Museum of Natural History—and Venice's only dinosaur skeleton.)

Just 100 yards ahead on the left (the tallest building with the red canopy), Venice's **Casinò** is housed in the palace where German composer Richard (*The Ring*) Wagner died in 1883. See his distinct, strong-jawed profile in the white plaque on the brick wall. In the 1700s, Venice was Europe's Vegas, with casinos and prostitutes everywhere. Casinòs ("little houses" in Venetian dialect) have long provided Italians with a handy escape from daily life. Today they're run by the state to keep Mafia influence at bay. Notice the fancy front porch, rolling out the red carpet for high rollers arriving by taxi or hotel boat.

Turkish "Fondaco" Exchange

San Stae Church

❹ San Stae

The San Stae Church sports a delightful Baroque facade. Opposite the San Stae stop is a little canal opening—on the second building to the right of that opening, look for the peeling plaster that once made up **frescoes** (you can barely distinguish the scant remains of little angels on the lower floors). Imagine the facades of the Grand Canal at their finest. Most of them would have been covered in frescoes by the best artists of the day. As colorful as the city is today, it's still only a faded, sepia-toned remnant of a long-gone era, a time of lavishly decorated, brilliantly colored palaces.

Just ahead (on the right, with blue posts) is the ornate white facade of **Ca' Pesaro,** which houses the International Gallery of Modern Art. *"Ca'"* is short for *casa* (house).

In this city of masks, notice how the rich marble facades along the Grand Canal mask what are generally just simple, no-nonsense brick buildings. Most merchants enjoyed showing off. However, being smart businessmen, they only decorated the side of the buildings that would be seen and appreciated. But look back as you pass Ca' Pesaro. It's the only building you'll see with a fine side facade. Ahead (about 100 yards on the left) is Ca' d'Oro, with its glorious triple-decker medieval arcade (just before the next stop).

❺ Ca' d'Oro

The lacy **Ca' d'Oro** (House of Gold) is the best example of Venetian Gothic architecture on the canal. Its three stories offer different variations on balcony design, topped with a spiny white roofline. Venetian Gothic mixes traditional Gothic (pointed arches and round medallions stamped with a four-leaf clover) with Byzantine styles (tall,

Ca' Pesaro—this *"ca'"* houses modern art

Ca' d'Oro—textbook Venetian Gothic

A *traghetto,* the poor man's gondola

Rialto Mercato hosts the fish market.

narrow arches atop thin columns), filled in with Islamic frills. Like all the palaces, this was originally painted and gilded to make it even more glorious than it is now. Today the Ca' d'Oro is an art gallery.

Look at the Venetian chorus line of palaces in front of the boat. On the right is the arcade of the covered **fish market,** with the open-air **produce market** just beyond. It bustles in the morning but is quiet the rest of the day. This is a great scene to wander through—even though European Union hygiene standards have made it cleaner but less colorful than it once was.

Find the *traghetto* gondola ferrying shoppers—standing like Washington crossing the Delaware—back and forth. There are three traghetto crossings along the Grand Canal, each one marked by a classy low-key green-and-black sign. Piloting a *traghetto* isn't these gondoliers' normal day jobs. As a public service, all gondoliers are obliged to row a traghetto a few days a month. Make a point to use them. At €2 a ride, *traghetti* offer the cheapest gondola rides in Venice (but at this price, don't expect them to sing to you).

❻ Rialto Mercato

This stop serves the busy market. The long, official-looking building at the stop is the Venice courthouse. Directly ahead (on the left) is the Fondaco dei Tedeschi (former German Exchange, a trading center for German merchants in the 16th century). It's now a luxury shopping mall with great rooftop views. Rising above it is the tip of the Campanile (bell tower), crowned by its golden angel weathervane at St. Mark's Square, where this tour will end.

You'll cruise by some trendy and beautifully situated wine bars

Rialto Bridge, with its 160-foot single span, marks Venice's traditional commercial neighborhood.

on the right, but look ahead as you round the corner and see the impressive Rialto Bridge come into view.

A major landmark, the **Rialto Bridge** is lined with shops and tourists. Constructed in 1588, it's the third bridge built on this spot. Until the 1850s, this was the only bridge crossing the Grand Canal. With a span of 160 feet and foundations stretching 650 feet on either side, the Rialto was an impressive engineering feat in its day. Earlier bridges here could open to let big ships in, but not this one. By the time this new bridge was completed, much of the Grand Canal was closed to shipping and became a canal of palaces.

When gondoliers pass under the fat arch of the Rialto Bridge, they take full advantage of its acoustics: "Volare, oh, oh..."

❼ Rialto

A separate town in the early days of Venice, Rialto has always been the commercial district, while San Marco was the religious and governmental center. Today, a winding street called the Mercerie connects the two, providing travelers with human traffic jams and a mesmerizing gauntlet of shopping temptations. This is the only stretch of the historic Grand Canal with landings upon which you can walk. Boats unloaded the city's basic necessities here: oil, wine, charcoal, iron. Today, the quay is lined with tourist-trap restaurants.

Venice's sleek, black, graceful **gondolas** are a symbol of the city (for more on gondolas, see page 198). With about 500 gondoliers joy-riding amid the churning vaporetti, there's a lot of congestion on the Grand Canal. Pay attention—this is where most gondola and vaporetto accidents take place. While the Rialto is the highlight of many gondola rides, gondoliers understandably prefer the quieter small canals. Watch your vaporetto driver curse the better-paid gondoliers.

Ahead 100 yards on the left, two gray-colored **palaces** stand side by side (City Hall and the mayor's office). Their horseshoe-shaped, arched windows are similar and their stories are the same height, lining up to create the effect of one long balcony.

❽ San Silvestro

We now enter a long stretch of important **merchants' palaces,** each with proud and different facades. Because ships couldn't navigate beyond the Rialto Bridge, the biggest palaces—with the major shipping needs—line this last stretch of the navigable Grand Canal.

Palaces like these were multi-functional: ground floor for the warehouse, offices and showrooms upstairs, and living quarters above, on the "noble floors" (with big windows to allow in maximum light). Servants lived and worked on the top floors (with the smallest windows). For fire-safety reasons, the kitchens were also located on the top floors. Peek into the noble floors to catch a glimpse of their still-glorious chandeliers of Murano glass.

Merchant's palace with water-level entries

Docking posts painted the family colors

❾ Sant'Angelo

Notice how many buildings have a foundation of waterproof white stone (*pietra d'Istria*) upon which the bricks sit high and dry. Many canal-level floors are abandoned as the rising water level takes its toll.

The **posts**—historically painted gaily with the equivalent of family coats of arms—don't rot underwater. But the wood at the waterline, where it's exposed to oxygen, does. On the smallest canals, little "no motorboats" signs indicate that these canals are for gondolas only (no motorized craft, 5 kph speed limit, no wake).

❿ San Tomà

Fifty yards ahead, on the right side (with twin obelisks on the rooftop) stands **Palazzo Balbi,** the palace of an early 17th-century captain general of the sea. This palace, like so many in the city, flies three flags: Italy (green-white-red), the European Union (blue with ring of stars), and Venice (a lion on a field of red and gold). Today it houses the administrative headquarters of the regional government.

Just past the admiral's palace, look immediately to the right, down a side canal. On the right side of that canal, before the bridge, see the traffic light and the **fire station** (the 1930s Mussolini-era building with four arches hiding fireboats parked and ready to go).

The impressive **Ca' Foscari,** with a classic Venetian facade (on the corner, across from the fire station), dominates the bend in the canal. This is the main building of the University of Venice, which has about 25,000 students. Notice the elegant lamp on the corner—needed in the old days to light this intersection.

The grand, heavy, white **Ca' Rezzonico,** just before the stop of the same name, houses the Museum of 18th-Century Venice (described on page 137). Across the canal is the cleaner and leaner **Palazzo Grassi,** the last major palace built on the canal, erected in the late 1700s. It was purchased by a French tycoon and now displays part of Punta della Dogana's contemporary art collection.

⓫ Ca' Rezzonico

Up ahead, the Accademia Bridge leads over the Grand Canal to the **Accademia Gallery** (right side), filled with the best Venetian paintings. There was no bridge here until 1854, when a cast-iron one was built. It was replaced with this wooden bridge in 1933. While meant to be temporary, it still stands today, nearly a century later.

Ca' Foscari, now part of the university

Ca' Rezzonico evokes 18th-century luxury.

⑫ Accademia

From here, look through the graceful bridge and way ahead to enjoy a classic view of **La Salute Church,** topped by a crown-shaped dome supported by scrolls. This Church of Saint Mary of Good Health was built to ask God to deliver Venetians from the devastating plague of 1630 (which had killed about a third of the city's population).

The low, white building among greenery (100 yards ahead, on the right, between the Accademia Bridge and the church) is the **Peggy Guggenheim Collection.** The American heiress "retired" here, sprucing up a palace that had been abandoned in midconstruction. Peggy willed the city her fine collection of modern art.

Two doors past the Guggenheim, Palazzo Dario has a great set of characteristic **funnel-shaped chimneys.** These forced embers through a loop-the-loop channel until they were dead—required in the days when stone palaces were surrounded by humble wooden buildings, and a live spark could make a merchant's workforce homeless. Three doors later is the **Salviati building,** which once served as a glassworks. Its fine Art Nouveau mosaic, done in the early 20th century, features Venice as a queen being appreciated by the big shots of society.

⑬ Santa Maria del Giglio

Back on the left stands the fancy **Gritti Palace hotel.** Hemingway and Woody Allen both stayed here (but not together).

Take a deep whiff of Venice. What's all this nonsense about stinky canals? All I smell is my shirt. By the way, how's your captain? Smooth dockings?

Accademia Bridge—great viewpoint and gateway to the art-filled Dorsoduro neighborhood

⓮ Salute

The huge **La Salute Church** towers overhead as if squirted from a can of Catholic Reddi-wip.

As the Grand Canal opens up into the lagoon, the last building on the right with the golden ball is the 17th-century **Customs House,** which now houses the Punta della Dogana contemporary art museum. Its two bronze Atlases hold a statue of Fortune riding the ball. Arriving ships stopped here to pay their tolls.

⓯ San Marco

Up ahead on the left, the green pointed tip of the Campanile marks **St. Mark's Square,** the political and religious center of Venice...and the final destination of this tour. You could get off at the San Marco stop and go straight to St. Mark's Square (and you'll have to if you're on vaporetto #2, which terminates here). But I'm staying on the #1 boat for one more stop, just past St. Mark's Square (it's a quick walk back).

Survey the lagoon. Opposite St. Mark's Square, across the water, the ghostly white church with the pointy bell tower is **San Giorgio Maggiore,** with great views of Venice. Next to it is the residential island Giudecca, stretching from close to San Giorgio Maggiore past

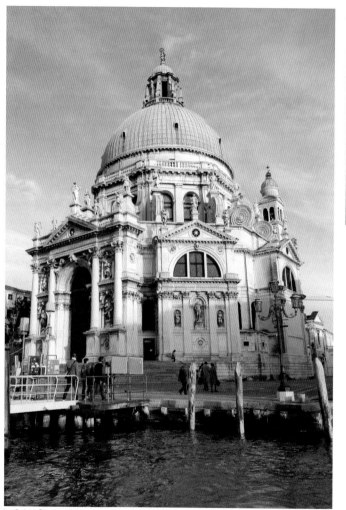

La Salute Church—its towering dome is topped with a statue of "Our Lady of Health"

the Venice youth hostel (with a nice view, directly across) to the Hilton Hotel (good nighttime view, far right end of island).

Still on board? If you are, as we leave the San Marco stop look left and prepare for a drive-by view of St. Mark's Square. First comes the bold white facade of the old mint (in front of the bell tower) marked by a tiny cupola, where Venice's golden ducat, the "dollar" of the Venetian Republic, was made, and the library facade, just three windows wide. Then come the twin columns, topped by St. Theodore and St. Mark, who've welcomed visitors since the 15th century. Between the columns, catch a glimpse of two giant figures atop the **Clock Tower**—they've been whacking their clappers every hour since 1499. The domes of **St. Mark's Basilica** are soon eclipsed by the lacy facade of the **Doge's Palace.** Next you'll see many gondolas with their green breakwater buoys, the **Bridge of Sighs** (leading from the palace to the prison—check out the maximum-security bars), and finally the grand harborside promenade—the **Riva.**

Follow the Riva with your eye, past elegant hotels to the green area in the distance. This is the largest of Venice's few **parks,** which hosts the annual Biennale festival (see page 148). Much farther in the distance is the **Lido,** the island with Venice's beach. Its sand and casinos are tempting, but given its car traffic, it lacks the medieval charm of Venice.

⑯ San Zaccaria

OK, you're at your last stop. Quick—muscle your way off this boat! (If you don't, you'll eventually end up at the Lido.)

At San Zaccaria, you're right in the thick of the action. A number of other vaporetti depart from here (see page 188). Otherwise, it's a short walk back along the Riva to St. Mark's Square. Ahoy!

St. Mark's Square Tour

Piazza San Marco

Venice was once Europe's richest city, and Piazza San Marco was its center. As middleman in the trade between Asia and Europe, wealthy Venice profited from both sides. In 1450, Venice had 180,000 citizens and a gross "national" product that exceeded that of entire countries.

The rich Venetians taught the rest of Europe about the good life—silks, spices, and jewels from the East; crafts from northern Europe; good food and wine; fine architecture, music, theater, and laughter. Venice was a vibrant city full of painted palaces, glittering canals, and impressed visitors. Five centuries after its power began to decline, Venice still has all of these, with the added charm of romantic decay. In this tour, we'll spend an hour in the heart of this Old World superpower.

ORIENTATION

Getting There: Signs all over town point to *San Marco*—meaning both the square and the basilica—located where the Grand Canal spills out into the lagoon. Vaporetto stops: San Marco or San Zaccaria.

Information: There's a TI in the southwest corner of St. Mark's Square.

Audio Tour: 🎧 You can download this chapter as a free Rick Steves audio tour (see page 193).

Services: Pay WCs are behind the Correr Museum and also at the waterfront park, Giardinetti Reali (near San Marco-Vallaresso vaporetto dock).

Eating: Cafés with live music provide an engaging soundtrack for St. Mark's Square (see "Cafés on St. Mark's Square" sidebar, later). The Correr Museum (at the end of the square opposite the basilica) has a quiet coffee shop overlooking the crowded square. For a list of restaurants in the area, see page 166.

Necessary Eyesores: Expect scaffolding and advertising billboards on monuments as a necessary part of long-term renovation projects.

Cardinal Points: The square is aligned (roughly) east-west. So, facing the basilica, north is to your left.

Starring: Byzantine domes, Gothic arches, Renaissance arches...and the wonderful, musical space they enclose.

Mark's winged lion appears everywhere.

St. Mark's Square makes the spirit soar.

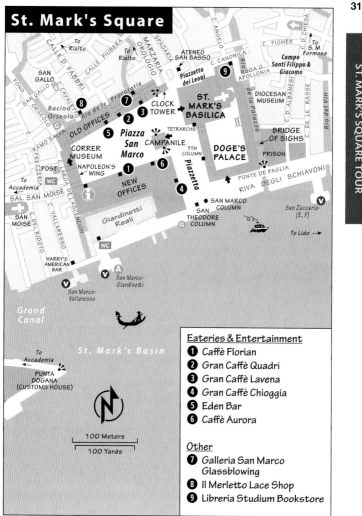

St. Mark's Square

Eateries & Entertainment
1. Caffè Florian
2. Gran Caffè Quadri
3. Gran Caffè Lavena
4. Gran Caffè Chioggia
5. Eden Bar
6. Caffè Aurora

Other
7. Galleria San Marco Glassblowing
8. Il Merletto Lace Shop
9. Libreria Studium Bookstore

100 Meters
100 Yards

THE TOUR BEGINS

▶ *For an overview of this grand square, view it from the west end of the square (away from St. Mark's Basilica).*

The Piazza

St. Mark's Basilica dominates the square with its Eastern-style onion domes and glowing mosaics. Mark Twain said it looked like "a vast warty bug taking a meditative walk." (I say it looks like tiara-wearing ladybugs copulating.) To the right of the basilica is its 325-foot-tall Campanile. Behind the Campanile, you can catch a glimpse of the pale-pink Doge's Palace. Lining the square are the former government offices (*procuratie*) that managed the treasury of St. Mark's, back when the church and state were one, and administered the Venetian empire's vast network of trading outposts, which stretched all the way to Turkey.

The square is big, but it feels intimate with its cafés and dueling orchestras. By day, it's great for people-watching and pigeon-chasing. By night, under lantern light, it transports you to another century, complete with its own romantic soundtrack. The piazza draws Indians in saris, English nobles in blue blazers, and Nebraskans in shorts.

With your back to the church, survey one of Europe's great urban spaces, and the only square in Venice to merit the title "Piazza." Nearly two football fields long, it's surrounded by the offices of the republic. One the right are the "old offices" (16th-century Renaissance). At left are the "new offices" (17th-century High Renaissance). Napoleon called the piazza "the most beautiful drawing room in Europe," and added to the intimacy by building the final wing, opposite the basilica, that encloses the square.

The arcade ringing the square, formerly lined with dozens of fine cafés, still provides an elegant promenade—complete with drapery that is dropped when necessary to provide relief from the sun.

Imagine this square full of water. That happens every so often at very high tides (*acqua alta*), a reminder that Venice and the sea are intertwined. (Now that one is sinking and the other is rising, they are more intertwined than ever.)

Venice became Europe's richest city from its trade with northern Europeans, Ottoman Muslims, and Byzantine Christians. Here in

St. Mark's Square, the exact center of this East-West axis, we see both the luxury and the mix of Eastern and Western influences.

Watch out for pigeon speckle. Venetians don't like pigeons but they do like seagulls—because they eat pigeons. In 2008, Venice outlawed the feeding of pigeons. But tourists—eager for a pigeon-clad photo op—haven't gotten that message. Vermin are also a problem on this small island, where it's said that each Venetian has two pigeons and four rats. (The rats stay hidden, except when high tides flood their homes.)

▸ *Now approach the basilica. If it's hot and you're tired, grab a shady spot at the foot of the Campanile.*

St. Mark's Basilica

The facade is a wild mix of East and West, with round, Roman-style arches over the doorways, golden Byzantine mosaics, a roofline ringed with pointed Gothic pinnacles, and Muslim-shaped onion domes (wood, covered with lead) on the roof. The brick-structure building is blanketed in marble that came from everywhere—columns from Alexandria, capitals from Sicily, and carvings from Constantinople. The columns flanking the doorways show the facade's variety—purple,

The piazza is magnificent whether floodlit or flooded—as it occasionally is at *acqua alta*.

Cafés on St. Mark's Square

In Venice's heyday, it was said that the freedoms a gentleman could experience here went far beyond what any true gentleman would actually care to indulge in. But one extravagance all could enjoy was the ritual of publicly consuming coffee: showing off with an affordable luxury, doing something trendy, while sharing the ideas of the Enlightenment.

Exotic coffee was made to order for the fancy café scene. Traders introduced coffee, called the "wine of Islam," from the Middle East (the plant is native to Ethiopia). The first coffeehouses opened in the 17th century, and by 1750 there were dozens of cafés lining Piazza San Marco and 200 operating in Venice.

Today, several fine old cafés survive and still line the square. Those with live music feature similar food, prices, and a three- to five-piece combo playing a selection of classical and pop hits, from Brahms to "Bésame Mucho."

You can wander around the square listening to the different orchestras, or take a seat at a café and settle in. At any café with live music, it's perfectly acceptable to nurse a cappuccino for an hour—you're paying for the music with the cover charge. And remember, you can sip your coffee at the bar at a nearly normal price—even with the orchestra playing just outside.

Caffè Florian (on the right as you face the church) is the most famous Venetian café and was one of the first places in Europe to serve coffee (daily 9:00-24:00, shorter hours off-season, www.caffeflorian.

green, gray, white, yellow, some speckled, some striped horizontally, some vertically, some fluted—all topped with a variety of different capitals.

What's amazing isn't so much the variety as the fact that the whole thing comes together in a bizarre sort of harmony. St. Mark's remains simply the most interesting church in Europe, a church that (to paraphrase Goethe) "can only be compared with itself."

For more on the basilica, inside and out, see the ✪ St. Mark's Basilica Tour chapter.

▶ *Facing the basilica, turn 90 degrees to the left to see the...*

com). It's been a popular spot for a discreet rendezvous in Venice since 1720. The orchestra plays a more classical repertoire compared to others on the square. The outside tables are the main action, but do walk inside through the richly decorated, old-time rooms where Casanova, Lord Byron, Charles Dickens, and Woody Allen have all paid too much for a drink.

Gran Caffè Quadri, opposite the Florian, has another illustrious roster of famous clientele.

Gran Caffè Lavena, near the Clock Tower, is less storied—although it dates from 1750 and counts composer Richard Wagner as a former regular. Drop in to check out its dazzling but politically incorrect chandelier.

Gran Caffè Chioggia, on the Piazzetta facing the Doge's Palace, charges no cover and has a few musicians playing—including a pianist. There's no inside ambience, but it's slightly cheaper than the others if you just want to sit on square.

Eden Bar and **Caffè Aurora** are less expensive and don't have live music.

Clock Tower (Torre dell'Orologio)

Any proper Renaissance city wanted to have a fine, formal entry and a clock tower. In Venice's case, its entry was visible from the sea and led from the big religious and governmental center to the rest of the city. The Clock Tower retains some of its original blue-and-gold pigments, a reminder that, in centuries past, this city glowed with bright color.

Two bronze "Moors" stand atop the Clock Tower (built originally to be Caucasian giants, they only switched their ethnicity when their metal darkened over the centuries). At the top of each hour they swing their giant clappers. The clock dial shows the 24 hours, the signs of the zodiac, and in the blue center, the phases of the moon—important

The Basilica's Byzantine-flavored domes

The Clock Tower's statues chime the hours.

information, as a maritime city with a shallow lagoon needs to know the tides. Above the dial is the world's first digital clock, which changes every five minutes.

An alert winged lion, the symbol of St. Mark and the city, looks down on the crowded square. He opens a book that reads *"Pax Tibi Marce,"* or "Peace to you, Mark." As legend goes, these were the comforting words that an angel spoke to the stressed evangelist, assuring him he would find serenity here on the island. Eventually, St. Mark's body found its final resting place inside the basilica, and now his winged-lion symbol is everywhere. (Find four in 20 seconds. Go.)

Venice's many lions express the city's various mood swings through history—triumphant after a naval victory, sad when a favorite son has died, hollow-eyed after a plague, and smiling when the soccer team wins. The pair of lions squatting between the Clock Tower and basilica have probably been photographed being ridden by every Venetian child born since the dawn of cameras.

Campanile

The original Campanile (cam-pah-NEE-lay, bell tower) was an observation tower and a marvel of medieval and Renaissance architecture until 1902, when it toppled into the center of the piazza. It had groaned ominously the night before, sending people scurrying from the cafés. The next morning...crash! The golden angel on top landed right at the basilica's front door, standing up.

The Campanile was rebuilt 10 years later complete with its golden archangel Gabriel, who always faces the breeze. You can ride a lift to the top for the best view of Venice. It's crowded at peak times, but well worth it (for Campanile hours, see page 129).

Because St. Mark's Square is the first place in town to start flooding, there are tide gauges at the outside base of the Campanile (near the exit, facing St. Mark's Square) that show the current sea level (*livello marea*). Find the stone plaque (near the exit door) that commemorates the high-water 77-inch level from the disastrous floods of 1966. In December 2008, Venice suffered another terrible high tide, cresting at 61 inches.

If the tide is mild (around 20 inches), the water merely seeps up through the drains. But when there's a strong tide (around 40 inches), it looks like someone's turned on a faucet down below. The water bubbles upward and flows like a river to the lowest points in the square, which can be covered with a few inches of water in an hour or so. When the water level rises one meter above mean sea level, a warning siren sounds, and it repeats if a serious flood is imminent.

Many doorways have three-foot-high wooden or metal barriers to block the high water (*acqua alta*), but the seawater still seeps in through floors and drains, rendering the barriers nearly useless.

You might see stacked wooden benches in the square; during floods, the benches are placed end-to-end to create elevated sidewalks. If you think the square is crowded now, when it's flooded it turns into total gridlock, as all the people normally sharing the whole square jostle for space on the narrow wooden walkways.

In 2006, the pavement around St. Mark's Square was taken up, and the entire height of the square was raised by adding a layer of sand, and then replacing the stones. If the columns along the ground floor of the Doge's Palace look stubby, it's because this process has been carried out many times over the centuries, buying a little more time as the sea slowly swallows the city.

Many generations have struck the same pose.

The Basilica's bell tower, or Campanile

Escape from St. Mark's Square

Crowds getting to you? Here are some relatively quiet areas on or near St. Mark's Square.

Correr Museum: Sip a cappuccino in the café of this uncrowded history museum in a building that overlooks St. Mark's Square (enter at the far end of the piazza). See page 127.

Giardinetti Reali: The small park is along the waterfront, west of the Piazzetta (facing the water, turn right—it's next to the TI and the only place near the square for a legal picnic).

San Giorgio Maggiore: This is the fairy-tale island you see from the Piazzetta (catch vaporetto #2 from the San Zaccaria-M.V.E. stop, past the Bridge of Sighs). See page 130.

Il Merletto: This lace shop is in a small, decommissioned chapel near the northwest corner of St. Mark's Square (daily 10:00-17:00, go through Sotoportego del Cavalletto and across the little bridge on the right). Ask for the sheet in English explaining the history of Venetian lace.

La Salute Church: This cool church in a quiet neighborhood is a short hop on vaporetto #1 from the San Marco-Vallaresso stop; or you can ride the nearby *traghetto*. See page 136.

Caffè Florian: The plush interior of this luxurious 18th-century café, located on St. Mark's Square, is generally quiet and nearly empty. A coffee here can be a wonderful break (see "Cafés on St. Mark's Square," earlier).

▶ *The small square between the basilica and the water is the...*

Piazzetta

This "Little Square" is framed by the Doge's Palace on the left, the library on the right, and the waterfront of the lagoon. In former days, the Piazzetta was closed to the public for a few hours a day so that government officials and bigwigs could gather in the sun to strike shady deals.

The pale-pink Doge's Palace is the epitome of the style known as Venetian Gothic. Columns support traditional, pointed Gothic arches, but with a Venetian flair—they're curved to a point, ornamented with a trefoil (three-leaf clover), and topped with a round medallion of a quatrefoil (four-leaf clover). The pattern is found on buildings all over Venice and on the formerly Venetian-controlled Croatian coast, but nowhere else in the world (except Las Vegas).

The two large 12th-century columns near the water were looted from Constantinople. Mark's winged lion sits on top of one. The lion's body (nearly 15 feet long) predates the wings and is more than 2,000 years old. The other column holds St. Theodore (battling a crocodile), the former patron saint who was replaced by Mark. I guess stabbing crocs in the back isn't classy enough for an upwardly mobile world power. Criminals were executed by being hung from these columns in the hopes that the public could learn its lessons vicariously.

Venice was the "Bride of the Sea" because she depended on sea trading for her livelihood. This "marriage" was celebrated annually by the people on Ascension Day. The doge, in full regalia, boarded a ritual boat (his Air Force One) here at the edge of the Piazzetta and sailed out into the lagoon. There a vow was made, and he dropped a jeweled ring into the water to seal the marriage.

In the distance, on an island across the lagoon, is the Church of San Giorgio Maggiore. This is one of the grandest views in the city. With its four tall columns as the entryway, the church, designed by the late-Renaissance architect Andrea Palladio, influenced the appearance of future government and bank buildings around the world.

Palladio's sober classical lines are pure and intellectual, but with their love of extravagance, Venetians wanted something more

The Piazzetta and the Doge's Palace

Venetian Gothic—arches and medallions

exuberant. More to local taste was the High Renaissance style of Jacopo Sansovino, who (around 1530) designed the library (here on the Piazzetta) and the delicate Loggetta at the base of the Campanile (destroyed by the collapse of the tower in 1902 and then pieced back together).

Tetrarchs and the Doge's Palace's Seventh Column

Where the basilica meets the Doge's Palace is the traditional entrance to the palace, decorated with four small Roman statues—the Tetrarchs. No one knows for sure who they are, but I like the legend that says they're the scared leaders of a divided Rome during its fall, holding their swords and each other as all hell breaks loose around them. Some believe that they are the leaders of the Eastern and Western empires (the bearded ones) with their chosen successors (the clean-shaven, younger ones). Whatever the legend, these statues—made of precious purple porphyry stone—are symbols of power. They were looted, likely from Constantinople, and then placed here proudly as spoils of war. How old are they? They've guarded the palace entrance since the city first rose from the mud.

About two-thirds of the way down the Doge's Palace, look for a column that's slightly shorter and fatter than the rest (the seventh from the water). Its carved capital tells a story of love, romance, and tragedy: 1) In the first scene (the carving facing the Piazzetta), a woman on a balcony is wooed by her lover, who says, "Babe, I want you!" 2) She responds, "Why, little ol' me?" 3) They get married. 4) Kiss. 5) Hit the sack—pretty racy for 14th-century art. 6) Nine months later, guess what? 7) The baby takes its first steps. 8) And as was all too common in the 1300s...the child dies.

For more on the Doge's Palace, see the ✪ Doge's Palace Tour chapter.

▸ *Continue down the Piazzetta to the waterfront. Turn left and walk (east) along the water. At the top of the first bridge, look inland at the...*

Bridge of Sighs

In the Doge's Palace (on your left), the government doled out justice. On your right are the prisons. (Don't let the palatial facade fool you—see the bars on the windows?) Prisoners sentenced in the palace crossed to the prisons by way of the covered bridge in front of you.

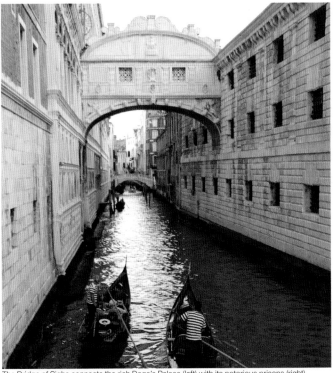

The Bridge of Sighs connects the rich Doge's Palace (left) with its notorious prisons (right).

This was called the Prisons' Bridge until the Romantic poet Lord Byron renamed it in the 19th century. From this bridge, the convicted got their final view of sunny, joyous Venice before entering the black and dank prisons. According to the Romantic legend, they sighed.

Venice has been a major tourist center for four centuries. Anyone who's ever come here has stood on this very spot, looking at the Bridge of Sighs. Lean on the railing leaned on by everyone from Casanova to Byron to Hemingway.

> *I stood in Venice, on the Bridge of Sighs,*
> *a palace and a prison on each hand.*
> *I saw, from out the wave, her structures rise,*
> *as from the stroke of the enchanter's wand.*
> *A thousand years their cloudy wings expand*
> *around me, and a dying glory smiles*
> *o'er the far times, when many a subject land*
> *looked to the Winged Lion's marble piles,*
> *where Venice sat in state, throned on her hundred isles!*

—from Lord Byron's *Childe Harold's Pilgrimage*

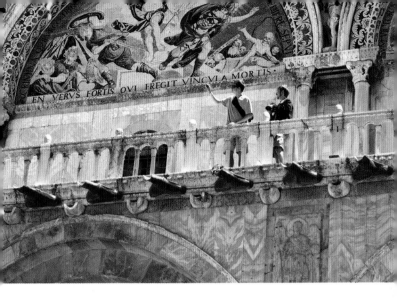

St. Mark's Basilica Tour

Basilica di San Marco

Among Europe's churches, St. Mark's is peerless. From the outside, it's a riot of domes, columns, and statues, completely unlike the towering Gothic churches of northern Europe or the heavy Baroque of much of the rest of Italy. Inside is a decor of mosaics, colored marbles, and oriental treasures that's rarely seen elsewhere. The Christian symbolism is unfamiliar to Western eyes, done in the style of Byzantine icons and even Islamic designs. Older than most of Europe's churches, it feels like a remnant of a lost world.

This is your best chance in Italy (outside of Ravenna) to glimpse a forgotten and somewhat mysterious part of the human story—Byzantium.

Cost: Free to enter church; €2 online reservation lets you skip the line. Three separate, optional sights inside charge admission: the Treasury (€3, includes audioguide), Golden Altarpiece (€2), and San Marco Museum—the sight most worth its entry fee (€5).

Hours: Church open Mon-Sat 9:45-17:00, Sun 14:00-17:00 (Sun until 16:00 Nov-Easter), interior brilliantly lit daily 11:30 to 12:30; museum open daily 9:45-16:45, including Sun mornings when the church itself is closed. The treasury and the Golden Altarpiece are both open Mon-Sat 9:45-17:00, Sun 14:00-17:00, Nov-Easter Mon-Sat until 16:00, Sun 14:00-16:00.

Reservations: You can book an entry time, even for the same day, for €2 at www.venetoinside.com (April-Oct only). You'll need your 17-digit confirmation number to enter.

Bag Check and Skipping the Line: Small purses and shoulder bags are usually allowed inside, but larger bags and backpacks are not. Check them for free for up to one hour at the nearby Ateneo San Basso church, 30 yards to the left of the basilica, down narrow Calle San Basso. Note that you generally can't check small bags that would be allowed inside. Those with a bag to check usually get to skip the line, as do their companions (meaning about one or two others—keep it within reason; this is at the guard's discretion). Leave your bag at Ateneo San Basso and pick up your claim tag. Take your tag to the basilica's tourist entrance. Keep to the left of the railing where the line forms and show your tag to the gatekeeper. He'll generally let you in, ahead of the line.

Dress Code: Modest dress (no bare knees or bare shoulders) is strictly enforced for men, women, and even kids. Shorts are OK if they cover the knees.

Information: Tel. 041-270-8311, www.basilicasanmarco.it.

Tours: Free, hour-long English tours (heavy on the mosaics' religious symbolism) are offered many days at 11:30 (meet in atrium).

St. Mark's Basilica

1. Exterior – Mosaic of Mark's Relics
2. Atrium – Mosaic of Noah's Ark & the Great Flood
3. Nave – Mosaics & Greek-Cross Floor Plan
4. Pentecost Mosaic
5. Central Dome – Ascension Mosaic
6. Rood Screen
7. Doge's Pulpit
8. Nicopeia Icon
9. Discovery of Mark Mosaic
10. Treasury
11. Golden Altarpiece
12. Stairs up to Museum

Audio Tour: 🎧 You can download this chapter as a free Rick Steves audio tour (see page 193).

Length of This Tour: Allow one hour.

WC: Inside the San Marco Museum.

Theft Alert: Watch for pickpockets in the jostling crowds.

Mass: Full services are outside of visiting hours (e.g., daily at 8:00 or 18:30; see www.basilicasanmarco.it for full schedule). Enter through the "worship only" door around the left side of the basilica.

Starring: St. Mark, Byzantium, mosaics, and ancient bronze horses.

THE TOUR BEGINS

▶ *Start outside in the square, far enough back to take in the whole facade. Then zero in on the details.*

❶ Exterior—Mosaic of Mark's Relics

St. Mark's Basilica is a treasure chest of booty that was looted during Venice's glory days. That's most appropriate for a church built on the stolen bones of a saint.

The **mosaic over the far left door** shows the theft that put Venice on the pilgrimage map. Two men (in the center, with crooked staffs) enter the church bearing a coffin with the body of St. Mark, who looks pretty grumpy from the long voyage.

St. Mark was the author of one of the Gospels, the four Bible books telling the story of Jesus' life (Matthew, Mark, Luke, and John). Eight centuries after his death, his holy body was in Muslim-occupied Alexandria, Egypt. In A.D. 828, two visiting merchants from Venice

St. Mark's—a church unlike any other

Mark's body is carried into the church.

"rescued" the body from the "infidels," hid it in a pork barrel (which was unclean to Muslims), and spirited it away to Venice.

The merchants presented the body—not to a pope or bishop, but to the doge (with white ermine collar, on the right) and his wife, the dogaressa (with entourage, on the left), giving instant status to Venice's budding secular state. They built a church here over Mark's bones and made him the patron saint of the city. You'll see his symbol, the winged lion, all over Venice.

The original church burned down in A.D. 976. Today's structure was begun in 1063. The mosaic, from 1260, shows that the church hasn't changed much since then—you can see the onion domes and famous bronze horses on the balcony.

St. Mark's was modeled after a great fourth-century church in Constantinople (Istanbul), giving upstart Venice an aura of tradition. In subsequent centuries, the church was encrusted with materials looted from buildings throughout the Venetian empire—bronze horses, plundered columns, and so on. The architectural style of St. Mark's has been called "Early Ransack."

▶ *Enter the atrium (entrance hall) of the basilica, through a sixth-century, bronze-paneled Byzantine door—which likely once swung in Constantinople's Hagia Sophia church. Immediately after being admitted by the dress-code guard, look up and to the right into an archway decorated with mosaics.*

❷ Atrium—Mosaic of Noah's Ark and the Great Flood

These are some of the oldest (13th century), finest, and most accessible mosaics in the church.

Atrium mosaic—Noah loads the ark

After the Flood, Noah releases a dove.

The nave—golden mosaics (on the ceiling), rood screen (midway down), and altar (far end)

Christ as Pantocrator

Most Eastern Orthodox churches have at least one mosaic or painting of Christ in a standard pose—as "Pantocrator," a Greek word meaning "Ruler of All." St. Mark's features several images of Christ as Pantocrator (especially the one in the central dome). The image, so familiar to Orthodox Christians, may be a bit foreign to Protestants, Catholics, and secularists.

As King of the Universe, Christ sits (usually on a throne) facing directly out, with penetrating eyes. He wears a halo divided with a cross. In his left hand is a Bible, while his right hand blesses, with the fingers forming the Greek letters chi and rho, the first two letters of "Christos." The thumb touches the fingers, symbolizing how Christ unites both his divinity and his humanity. On either side of Christ's head are the Greek letters "IC XC," short for "IesuC XristoC."

In the scene to the right of the entry door, Noah and sons are sawing logs to build a boat. Venetians—who were great ship builders—related to the story of Noah and the Ark. At its peak, Venice's Arsenale warship-building plant employed several thousand. Below that are three scenes of Noah putting all species of animals into the Ark, two by two. (Who's at the head of the line? Lions.) Across the arch, the Flood hits in full force, drowning the wicked. Noah sends out a dove twice to see whether there's any dry land where he can dock. He finds it, leaves the Ark with a gorgeous rainbow overhead, and offers a sacrifice of thanks to God.

▶ *Rejoin the slow flow of people. Notice the entrance to the San Marco Museum (Loggia dei Cavalli), which we'll visit later. Now climb seven steps, pass through the doorway, and enter the nave. Loiter somewhere just inside the door (crowd permitting) and let your eyes adjust.*

❸ The Nave—Mosaics and Greek-Cross Floor Plan

The initial effect is dark and unimpressive (unless they've got the floodlights on). But as your pupils slowly unclench, notice that the entire upper part is decorated in mosaic—nearly 5,000 square yards (imagine paving a football field with contact lenses). These golden mosaics are in the Byzantine style, though many were designed by artists

Mosaics

St. Mark's mosaics are designs or pictures made with small cubes of colored stone or glass pressed into wet plaster. Ancient Romans paved floors, walls, and ceilings with them. When Rome "fell," the art form died out in the West but was carried on by Byzantine craftsmen. They perfected the gold background effect by baking gold leaf into tiny cubes of glass called *tesserae* (tiles). The surfaces of the tiles are purposely cut unevenly to capture light and give off a shimmering effect. The reflecting gold mosaics helped to light thick-walled, small-windowed, lantern-lit Byzantine churches, creating a golden glow that symbolized the divine light of heaven.

St. Mark's mosaics tell the entire Christian history from end to beginning— from the Apocalypse near the entrance to Christ's Old Testament origins near the altar. At either end are images of Christ—the beginning and the end, the Alpha and Omega of the Christian universe.

from the Italian Renaissance and later. The often-overlooked lower walls are covered with green-, yellow-, purple-, and rose-colored marble slabs, cut to expose the grain, and laid out in geometric patterns. Even the floor is mosaic, with mostly geometrical designs. It rolls like the sea. Venice is sinking and shifting, creating these cresting waves of stone.

The church is laid out with four equal arms, topped with domes, radiating out from the center to form a Greek cross (+). The Greek-cross floor plan symbolizes perfection, rather than the more common Latin cross of the crucifixion (emphasizing man's sinfulness).

Those familiar with Eastern Orthodox churches will find familiar elements in St. Mark's: a central floor plan, domes, mosaics, and iconic images of Mary and Christ as Pantocrator—ruler of all things. As your eyes adjust, the mosaics start to give off a "mystical, golden luminosity," the atmosphere of the Byzantine heaven. The air itself seems almost visible, like a cloud of incense. It's a subtle effect, one that grows on you as the filtered light changes. There are more beautiful, bigger, more overwhelming, and even holier churches, but none is as stately.

▶ *Find the chandelier near the entrance doorway (in the shape of a Greek-cross cathedral space station), and run your eyes up the support chain to the dome above.*

❹ Pentecost Mosaic

In a golden heaven, the dove of the Holy Spirit shoots out a pinwheel of spiritual lasers, igniting tongues of fire on the heads of the 12 apostles below, giving them the ability to speak other languages without a Rick Steves phrase book. You'd think they'd be amazed, but their expressions are as solemn as...icons. One of the oldest mosaics in the church (c. 1125), it has distinct "Byzantine" features: a gold background and apostles with halos, solemn faces, almond eyes, delicate blessing hands, and rumpled robes, all facing forward.

This is art from a society still touchy about the Bible's commandment against making "graven images" of holy things. The Byzantine style emphasizes otherworldliness rather than literal human detail.

Ascension Mosaic—12 Apostles and Mary ring the dome beneath Christ in heaven

▶ *Shuffle along with the crowds up to the central dome.*

❺ Central Dome—Ascension Mosaic

Gape upward to the very heart of the church. Christ—having lived his miraculous life and having been crucified for man's sins—ascends into the starry sky on a rainbow. He raises his right hand and blesses the universe. This isn't the dead, crucified, mortal Jesus featured in most churches, but a powerful, resurrected god, the ruler of all.

Christ's blessing radiates, rippling down to the ring of white-robed apostles below. They stand amid the trees of the Mount of Olives, waving good-bye as Christ ascends. Mary is with them, wearing blue with golden Greek crosses on each shoulder and looking ready to play patty-cake. From these saints, goodness descends, creating the Virtues that ring the base of the dome between the windows. In Byzantine churches, the window-lit dome represented heaven, while the dark church below represented earth—a microcosm of the hierarchical universe.

Beneath the dome at the four corners, the four Gospel writers ("Matev," "Marc," "Luca," and "Ioh") thoughtfully scribble down the heavenly events. This wisdom flows down like water from the symbolic Four Rivers below them, spreading through the church's four equal arms (the "four corners" of the world), and baptizing the congregation with God's love. The church building is a series of perfect circles within perfect squares—the cosmic order—with Christ in the center solemnly blessing us. God's in his heaven, saints are on earth, and all's right with the world.

Look around at the church's furniture and imagine a service here. The ❻ **rood screen,** (like the iconostasis in a Greek church) topped with 14 saints, separates the congregation from the high altar, heightening the "mystery" of the Mass. The ❼ **pulpit on the right** was reserved for the doge, who led prayers and made important announcements.

The Venetian church service is a theatrical multimedia spectacle, combining words, music, images (mosaics), costumes (priests' robes), props (candles, incense), set design (rood screen), and even stage direction (processionals through the crowd). Coincidentally or not, the first modern opera—also a multimedia theatrical experience—was written by St. Mark's *maestro di cappella,* Claudio Monteverdi (1567-1643).

Byzantium, the Fourth Crusade, and Venice

The Byzantine Empire was the eastern half of the ancient Roman Empire that *didn't* "fall" in A.D. 476. It remained Christian, Greek-speaking, and enlightened for another thousand years.

In A.D. 330, Constantine, the first Christian emperor, moved the Roman Empire's capital to the newly expanded city of Byzantium, which he humbly renamed Constantinople. Venice had strong ties with Byzantium from its earliest days. Venetian merchants were granted trading rights to Byzantine ports in the Adriatic and eastern Mediterranean. They traded raw materials from Western Europe for luxury goods from the East. As Venice grew more powerful, they wanted still more access to Byzantium's wealth. In the year 1204, they saw their chance. They joined the pope's Crusade to "save" the Holy Land from Muslim influence. But along the way, the ships diverted to Constantinople. The doge-led Crusaders sacked the Byzantine capital and brought the booty home to Venice. In St. Mark's Basilica, you can see these treasures: the bronze horses, bronze doors of Hagia Sophia, Golden Altarpiece enamels, the Treasury's treasures, the Nicopeia icon, and much of the marble that now covers the (brick) church.

Byzantine Empire

Venice
Genoa
Ravenna
Pisa
Rome
Constantinople
Nicaea
Athens
Antioch
Jerusalem

= Empire

Mosaics, like this Last Supper, use gold backgrounds to reflect light in the dim church interior.

North Transept

In the north transept (the arm of the church to the left of the altar), today's Venetians pray to a painted wooden icon of Mary and Baby Jesus known as ❽ **Nicopeia,** or "Our Lady of Victory." It's on the east wall of the north transept, a small painting crusted over with a big stone canopy. In its day, this was the ultimate trophy—the actual icon used to protect the Byzantine army in war, looted by the Crusaders. Supposedly painted by the evangelist Luke, it was once enameled with bright paint and precious stones, and Mary was adorned with a crown and necklace of gold and jewels (now on display in the Treasury). Now the protector of Venetians, this Madonna has helped the city persevere through plagues, wars, and crucial soccer games.

▶ *In the south transept (to the right of the main altar), find the dim mosaic high up on the three-windowed wall.*

❾ Discovery of Mark Mosaic

It's 1094, the church is nearly complete (see the domes shown in cutaway fashion), and they're all set to re-inter Mark's bones under the new altar. There's just one problem: During the decades of construction, they forgot where they'd stored his body!

So (on the left half), all of Venice gathers inside the church to bow down and pray for help finding the bones. The doge (from the Latin *dux,* meaning "leader") leads them. Soon after (on the right), the patriarch (far right) is inspired to look inside a hollow column where he finds the relics. Everyone turns and applauds, including the womenfolk (left side of scene), who stream in from the upper-floor galleries. The relics were soon placed under the altar in a ceremony that inaugurated the current structure.

Nearby, the door under the rose window, with the green curtain, leads directly from the Doge's Palace. On important occasions, the doge entered the church through here, ascended the steps of his pulpit, and addressed the people.

▶ *The two-room Treasury is in the south transept.*

❿ Treasury (Tesoro)

The Treasury holds an amazing collection of precious items, most of them stolen from Constantinople: Byzantine chalices, silver reliquaries, monstrous monstrances (for displaying the Communion wafer), and icons done in gold, silver, enamels, gems, and semiprecious stones. As Venice thought of itself as the granddaughter of Rome and the daughter of Byzantium, Venetians consider these treasures not stolen, but inherited. This is marvelous handiwork, but all the more marvelous for having been done when Western Europe was still mired in mud.

▶ *Enter the main room, to the right. Start with the large glass case in the center of the room.*

Main Room: In the display case, the hanging lamp with the protruding fish features fourth-century Roman rock crystal framed in 11th-century Byzantine metalwork. In fact, several Treasury items

As this mosaic over the church door shows, St. Mark's looks today much as it did 800 years ago.

The Legend of St. Mark

Mark (died c. A.D. 68) was a Jewish-born Christian, and he might have actually met Jesus. He traveled with fellow convert Paul, eventually settling in Alexandria as the city's first Christian bishop. On a trip to Rome, Peter—Jesus' right-hand man—asked him to write down the events of Jesus' life. This became the Gospel of Mark.

During his travels, Mark stopped in the lagoon (in Aquileia on the north coast of the Adriatic), where he dreamed of a Latin-speaking angel who said, *"Pax tibi Marce, evangelista meus"* ("Peace to you, Mark, my evangelist"), promising him rest after death. Back in Alexandria, Mark was attacked by an anti-Christian mob. They tied him with ropes and dragged his body through the streets until he died.

Eight centuries later, his body lay in an Alexandrian church that was about to be vandalized by Muslim fanatics. Two Venetian traders on a business trip saved the relics from desecration by hiding them in a pork barrel—a meat considered unclean by Muslims—and quickly setting sail. The perilous voyage home was only completed after many more miracles. The doge received the body, and in 828 they built the first church of St. Mark to house it. During construction of the current church (1094), Mark's relics were temporarily lost, and it took another miracle to find them, hidden inside a column. Today, Venetians celebrate Mark on the traditional date of his martyrdom, April 25.

represent the fruits of labor by different civilizations over a thousand-year period.

Just behind the lamp, a black bucket, carved with scenes of satyrs chasing nymphs, epitomizes the pagan world that was fading as Christianity triumphed. Also in the case are blue-and-gold lapis lazuli icons of the Crucifixion and of the Archangel Michael—standing like an action hero, ready to conquer evil in the name of Christ. See various chalices made of onyx, agate, and rock crystal, and an incense burner shaped like a domed church.

▶ *Along the walls, find the following displays (working counterclockwise around the room).*

The first three glass cases have bowls and urns from the three medieval cultures that cross-pollinated in the Eastern Mediterranean: Venetian, Byzantine, and Islamic. Next, on a wooden pedestal, comes the Urn of Artaxerxes I (next to window in the right wall), an Egyptian-made object that once held the ashes of the great Persian king who ruled 2,500 years ago (r. 465-425 B.C.). The next cases hold religious paraphernalia used for High Mass, including the 600-year-old crosier (shepherd staff) still used today on holy days.

Next is the small marble Ciborio di Anastasia (far left corner). It may be a gift from "Anastasia," the name carved on it in Greek. She was a lady-in-waiting in the court of the Byzantine emperor Justinian (483-565). Legend has it she was so beautiful that Justinian (a married man) pursued her amorously, so she had to dress like a monk and flee to a desert monastery.

Moving to the next wall, you'll see two large golden altarpiece panels, flanked by two golden candlesticks with amazing detail—from the smiling angels on top all the way down to the roots. Continuing counterclockwise, notice how the granite column extends below current floor level, as things have settled over the last 1,000 years.

Continue into the relics room. The glass case over the glowing alabaster altar contains a reliquary showing Christ being whipped (from 1125). It holds a stone (supposedly) from the column he was tied to.

▶ *The Golden Altarpiece is located behind the main altar. Join the line to pay, and then go through the turnstile.*

⓫ Golden Altarpiece (Pala d'Oro)

Under the green marble canopy, supported by four intricately carved alabaster columns, sits the high altar. Inside the altar is an urn (not visible) with the mortal remains of Mark, the Gospel writer. (Look through the grate of the altar to read *Corpus Divi Marci Evangelistae*, or "Body of the Evangelist Mark.") He rests in peace, as an angel had promised him. Shh.

The Golden Altarpiece itself is a stunning golden wall made of 250 blue-backed enamels with religious scenes, all set in a gold frame and

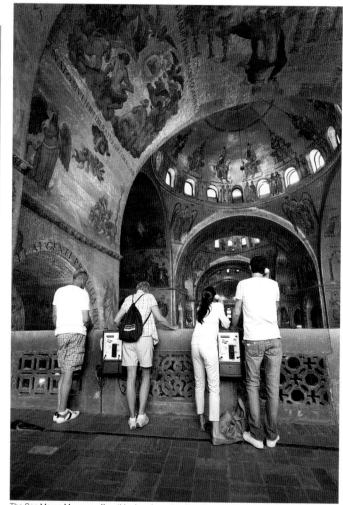

The San Marco Museum offers this view down the church nave, with its Pentecost mosaic.

studded with 15 hefty rubies, 300 emeralds, 1,500 pearls, and assorted sapphires, amethysts, and topaz. The Byzantine-made enamels were part of the Venetians' plunder of 1204, subsequently pieced together by Byzantine craftsmen specifically for St. Mark's high altar. It's a bit much to take in all at once, but get up close and find several details you might recognize:

In the center of it all, Jesus sits on a golden throne, with a halo of pearls and jewels. Like a good Byzantine Pantocrator, he dutifully faces forward and gives his blessing while stealing a glance offstage at Mark ("Marcus") and the other saints.

Along the bottom row, Old Testament prophets show off the books of the Bible they've written. With halos, solemn faces, and elaborately creased robes, they epitomize the Byzantine icon style.

Mark's story is depicted in the panels along the sides. In the bottom left panel, Mark meets Peter (seated) at the gates of Rome, to receive his call. In the bottom right panel, the two Venetian merchants return by ship, carrying Mark's coffin here to be laid to rest.

Byzantium excelled in the art of *cloisonné* enameling: A piece of gold leaf is stamped with a design, then filled in with pools of enamel paint, which are baked on. Some saints even have pearl crowns or jewel collars pinned on. This kind of craftsmanship—and the social infrastructure that could afford it—made Byzantium seem like an enchanted world during Europe's dim Middle Ages.

After you've looked at some individual scenes, back up as far as this small room will let you and just let yourself be dazzled by the whole picture—this "mosaic" of Byzantine greatness. This magnificent altarpiece sits on a swivel (as you can see) and is swung around on festival Sundays so the entire congregation can enjoy it, as Venetians have for so many centuries.

⑫ San Marco Museum (Museo di San Marco)

▶ *The steep staircase up to the museum is in the atrium near the main entrance. The sign says* Loggia dei Cavalli, Museo. *Ascend the steps, buy your ticket, and enter. In the first room, you'll see several models of the church at various stages of its history. Notice how the original domes, once squat, were made taller in the 13th century, leaving today's church with a dome-within-a-dome structure.*

Next are the museum's three highlights: view of the interior (right), view of the square (out the door to the left), and bronze horses (directly ahead). Belly up to the stone balustrade (on the right) to survey the interior.

View of Church Interior

Scan the church, with its thousands of square meters of mosaics, then take a closer look at the Pentecost mosaic (first dome above you, described earlier). The unique design at the very top signifies the Trinity: throne (God), Gospels (Christ), and dove (Holy Spirit). The couples below the ring of apostles are the people of the world (I can find Judaea, Cappadocia, and Asia), who, despite their different languages, still understood the Spirit's message.

If you were a woman in medieval Venice, you'd enjoy this same close-up view. The balcony was for women, the nave for men, and the altar for the priests. Back then the rood screen (the fence with the 15 figures on it) separated the priest from the public. Looking down at the nave, appreciate the patterns of the mosaic floor—one of the finest in Italy.

▶ *From here, the museum loops you along the left gallery to the far (altar) end of the church, then back to the bronze horses. Along the way, you'll see…*

Mosaic Fragments

These mosaics once hung in the church, but when they became damaged or aesthetically old-fashioned, they were replaced by new and more fashionable mosaics. You'll see mosaics from the church's earliest days (and most "Byzantine" style, c. 1070) to more recent times (1700s, more realistic and detailed). Many are accompanied by small photos that show how the remaining fragment once fit into a larger scene.

The mosaics—made from small cubes of stone or colored glass pressed into wet clay—were assembled on the ground, then cemented onto the walls. Artists draw the pattern on paper, lay it on the wet clay, and slowly cut the paper away as they replace it with cubes.

▶ *Continuing on, down a set of stairs, you'll catch glimpses of the interior of the church from the north transept. Here you get a close-up view of the Tree of Jesse mosaic, showing Jesus' distant ancestor at the root and his mom at the top. Continue on to the Sala dei Banchetti (WCs and a vending machine with drinks near the room's entrance).*

Sala dei Banchetti

This large, ornate room—once the doge's banquet hall—is filled with religious objects, tapestries and carpets that once adorned the church, Burano-made lace vestments, illuminated music manuscripts, a doge's throne, and much more. In the center of the hall stands the most prestigious artwork here, the Pala Feriale, by Paolo Veneziano (1345), with scenes from Mark's life.

▶ *Now double back toward the museum entrance, through displays of stone fragments from the church, finally arriving at...*

The Bronze Horses (La Quadriga)

Stepping lively in pairs and with smiles on their faces, they exude energy and exuberance. Art historians don't know how old they are—they could be from ancient Greece (fourth century B.C.) or from ancient Rome, during its Fall (fourth century A.D.). Professor Carbon Fourteen says they're from around 175 B.C. Originally, the horses pulled a chariot driven by an emperor, *Ben-Hur* style.

These bronze statues were not hammered and bent into shape by metalsmiths, but were cast from clay molds using what is called the lost-wax technique. The heads are detachable and adjustable—even swappable. The bronze is high quality, with 97 percent copper.

One of the treasures of the ancient world, this group has inspired Caesars, kings, and doges.

Originally gilded, they still have some streaks of gold. Long gone are the ruby pupils that gave the horses the original case of "red eye." While four-horse statues were once relatively common, this is the only intact group of four horses to survive from ancient times. That they survived at all is amazing, as bronze work like this almost always ends up being smelted down by conquerors.

Megalomaniacs through the ages have coveted these horses not only for their artistic value, but because they symbolize Apollo, the Greco-Roman god of the sun...and of secular power. Legend says they were made in the time of Alexander the Great, then taken by Nero to Rome. Constantine took them to his new capital in Constantinople to adorn the chariot racecourse. The Venetians then stole them from their fellow Christians when they sacked the city in 1204 and brought them here to St. Mark's in 1255. The church's atrium was built as a pedestal for the horses. The doge spoke to his people standing between the horses when they graced the balcony atop the church's facade (where the copies—which you'll see next—stand today).

What goes around comes around, and Napoleon came around and took the horses when he conquered Venice in 1797. They stood atop a triumphal arch in Paris until Napoleon's empire was "blown-aparte"

The Bronze Horse copies enjoy a stunning view of the Piazza, as part of the San Marco Museum.

and they were returned to their "rightful" home. Their expressive faces seem to say, "Oh boy, Wilbur, have we done some travelin'."

In 1975, the horses were again removed from their spot when they were attacked by their most dangerous enemy yet—the threat of oxidation from pollution, which sent them galloping for cover inside the church.

▶ *The visit ends outside on the balcony overlooking St. Mark's Square.*

The Loggia and View of St. Mark's Square

You'll be drawn repeatedly to the viewpoint of the square, but remember to look at the facade to see how cleverly all the looted architectural elements blend together. Ramble among the statues of water-bearing slaves that serve as drain spouts. The horses are modern copies (note the 1978 date on the hoof of the horse to the right).

Be a doge, and stand between the bronze horses overlooking St. Mark's Square—under the gilded lion of St. Mark, in front of the four great Evangelists, and flanked by the four glorious horses. Admire the mesmerizing, commanding view of the city, which so long ago was Europe's only superpower, and today is just a small town with a big history.

Doge's Palace Tour

Palazzo Ducale

Venice is a city of beautiful facades—palaces, churches, carnival masks—that can cover darker interiors of intrigue and decay. The Doge's Palace, with its frilly pink exterior, hides the fact that the "Most Serene Republic" (as Venice called itself) was far from serene in its heyday.

The Doge's Palace housed the fascinating government of this rich and powerful empire. It also served as the home for the Venetian ruler known as the doge (pronounced "dohzh"), or duke. For four centuries (about 1150-1550), this was the most powerful half-acre in Europe. The doges wanted their palace to reflect the wealth and secular values of the Republic, impressing visitors and serving as a reminder that the Venetians were Number One in Europe.

ORIENTATION

Cost: €20 combo-ticket includes the Correr Museum, also covered by Museum Pass.

Hours: Daily 8:30-19:00, Nov-March until 17:30, last entry one hour before closing.

Avoiding Lines: Avoid the long peak-season line at the Doge's Palace by buying your combo-ticket (or Museum Pass) at the uncrowded Correr Museum. This lets you enter the Doge's Palace at the "pre-paid tickets" entrance. You can also get prepaid tickets 48 hours in advance online. Crowds tend to diminish after 15:00.

Getting There: The palace is next to St. Mark's Basilica, on the lagoon waterfront, and just off St. Mark's Square. Vaporetto stops: San Marco or San Zaccaria.

Information: Tel. 041-271-5911, http://palazzoducale.visitmuve.it.

Tours: The audioguide (€5, must leave ID) is dry but informative. The fine 1.25-hour Secret Itineraries guided tour lets you skip the line and covers rooms otherwise not open to the public (€20, wise to reserve ahead: from the US dial 011-39-041-4273-0892, within Italy call 848-082-000, book online, or try just showing up at the info desk). Avoid the Doge's Hidden Treasures Tour—it reveals little that would be considered a "treasure."

Length of This Tour: Allow 1.5 hours.

Services: WCs are in the courtyard and halfway up the stairs to balcony level. Bags bigger than a large purse must be checked (free).

Cuisine Art: A pricey sandwich-and-salad café is off the palace courtyard.

Starring: Big rooms bare of furnishings but crammed with history, Tintoretto masterpieces, and the doges.

Doge's Palace

To Rialto

CALLE CANONICA

Campo
SS Filippo &
Giacomo

PIAZZETTA
DEI LEONI

RUGA GIUFFA
S. APOLLONIA

To San
Zaccaria

50 Meters

50 Yards

CLOCK
TOWER

ST.
MARK'S
BASILICA

Rio de Palazzo

Piazza
San
Marco

TETRARCHS

STAIRWAY
OF GIANTS

❶

❷

BRIDGE
OF SIGHS

PORTA
DELLA
CARTA
(EXIT)

GOLDEN
STAIRCASE

❸

NEW
PRISON

CAMPANILE

Courtyard

DOGE'S
PALACE

NEW
OFFICES

Piazzetta

❹

PONTE
DELLA
PAGLIA

RIVA DEGLI
SCHIAVONI

CALLE DEL ALBANESI

To

SAN
MARCO
COLUMN

ENTRY

TOUR BEGINS

SAN
THEODORE
COLUMN

San Zaccaria

V

To Vaporetto
& WC

St. Mark's
Basin

DOGE'S PALACE TOUR

❶ Doge's Apartments
(1st Floor)

❷ Executive & Legislative Rooms
(3rd Floor)

❸ Judicial Rooms & Armory
Museum (3rd Floor)

❹ Hall of the Grand Council
(3rd Floor)

THE TOUR BEGINS

Exterior

"The Wedding Cake," "The Tablecloth," or "The Pink House" is also sometimes known as the Doge's Palace. The style is called Venetian Gothic—a fusion of Italian Gothic with a delicate Islamic flair. The columns originally had bases on the bottoms, but these were covered over as the columns sank through the centuries.

The palace was originally built in the 800s, but most of what we see came after 1300, as it was expanded to meet the needs of the empire. Each doge wanted to leave his mark on history with a new wing.

If you compare this lacy, top-heavy structure with the massive fortress palaces of Florence, you realize the wisdom of building a city in the middle of the sea—you have no natural enemies except gravity. This unfortified palace in a city with no city wall was the doge's way of saying, "I am an elected and loved ruler. I do not fear my own people."

▶ *Enter the Doge's Palace from along the waterfront. After you pass through the turnstile, ignore the signs and cross to the far side of the courtyard. Stand at the foot of the grand staircase topped by two statues.*

The Courtyard and the Stairway of Giants (Scala dei Giganti)

Imagine yourself as a foreign dignitary on business to meet the doge. In the courtyard, you look up a grand staircase topped with two nearly nude statues of, I think, Moses and Paul Newman (more likely, Neptune and Mars, representing Venice's prowess at sea and at war). The doge and his aides would be waiting for you at the top, between

Lacy, unfortified home of the doge

Grand entrance guarded by Neptune and Mars

Mouth of Truth—the post box of doom

Golden Staircase with a 24-carat ceiling

the two statues and beneath the winged lion. No matter who you were—king, pope, or emperor—you'd have to hoof it up. The powerful doge would descend the stairs for no one.

Many doges were crowned here, between the two statues. The doge was something like an elected king—which makes sense only in the dictatorial republic that was Venice. Technically, he was just a noble selected by other nobles to carry out their laws and decisions. Many doges tried to extend their powers and rule more as divine-right kings. Many others just put on their funny hats and accepted their role as figurehead and ceremonial ribbon cutter.

The palace is attached to the church, symbolically welding church and state. Both buildings have ugly brick behind a painted-lady veneer of marble. In this tour, we'll see the similarly harsh inner workings of an outwardly serene, polished republic.

▶ *Cross back to near the entrance and follow the signs up the tourists' staircase to the first-floor balcony (loggia). Midway along the balcony, you'll find a face in the wall, the...*

Mouth of Truth

This fierce-looking androgyne opens his/her mouth, ready to swallow a piece of paper, hungry for gossip. Letterboxes like this (some with lions' heads) were scattered throughout the palace. Originally, anyone who had a complaint or suspicion about anyone else could accuse him anonymously (*denontie secrete*) by simply dropping a slip of paper in the mouth. This set the blades of justice turning inside the palace.

▶ *A few steps toward Paul Newman is the entrance to the...*

Paintings by Titian, Veronese, and Tintoretto

The doge had only the top Venetian painters decorate his palace. While the palace was once rich in Titians, fires in the late 1500s destroyed nearly all the work by the greatest Venetian master. As the palace was reconstructed, the Titians were replaced with works by Veronese and Tintoretto. Most are canvases—not murals or frescoes—painted in workshops and hung on the walls.

Veronese used the best pigments available—from precious stones, sapphires, and emeralds—and his colors have survived vividly. These Veronese paintings are by his hand and are fine examples of his genius. Tintoretto, on the other hand, didn't really have his heart in these commissions, and the pieces here were done by his workshop.

The paintings of the Doge's Palace are a study of old Venice, with fine views of the old city and its inhabitants. The extravagant women's gowns in the paintings by Veronese show off a major local industry—textiles. While the paintings are not generally of masterpiece quality, they're historically interesting. They prove that in the old days, Venice had no pigeons.

Golden Staircase (Scala d'Oro)

The palace was architectural propaganda, designed to impress visitors. This 24-karat gilded-ceiling staircase was something for them to write home about. As you ascend the stairs, look back at the floor below and marvel at its 3-D pattern.

▶ *Start up the first few steps of the Golden Staircase. Midway up, at the first landing, turn right, which takes you up into the...*

Doge's Apartments (Appartamento del Doge)

The dozen or so rooms on the first floor are where the doge actually lived. The blue-and-gold-hued Sala dei Scarlatti (Room 5) is typical of the palace's interior decoration: gold-coffered ceiling, big stone fireplace, silky walls with paintings, and a speckled floor. There's very little original furniture, as doges were expected to bring their own. Despite his high office, the doge had to obey several rules that bound him to the city. He couldn't leave the palace unescorted, he couldn't open official mail in private, and he and his family had to leave their own home and live in the Doge's Palace.

The large Room 6, the Sala dello Scudo (Shield Hall), is full of maps and globes. The main map illustrates the reach of Venice's maritime realm, which stretched across most of the eastern Mediterranean. With the maps in this room you can trace the eye-opening trip across Asia—from Italy to Greece to Palestine, Arabia, and "Irac"—of local boy Marco Polo (c. 1254-1325). Finally, he arrived at the other side of the world. This last map (at the far end of the room) is shown "upside-down," with south on top, giving a glimpse of the Venetian worldview circa 1550. It depicts China, Taiwan (Formosa), and Japan (Giapan), while America is a nearby island with California and lots of Terre Incognite.

In Room 7, the Sala Grimani, are several paintings of the lion of St. Mark, including the famous one by Vittore Carpaccio of a smiling lion (on the long wall). The lion holds open a book with these words, *"Pax Tibi Marce..."* ("Peace to you, Mark"), which, according to legend, were spoken by an angel welcoming St. Mark to Venice. In the background is the Doge's Palace and the Campanile.

▶ *Finish browsing the dozen or so private rooms of the Doge's Apartments, and continue up the Golden Staircase to the third floor, which was the "public" part of the palace. The room right at the top of the stairs is the...*

Square Room (Atrio Quadrato)

The ceiling painting, **Justice Presenting the Sword and Scales to Doge Girolamo Priuli,** is by Tintoretto. (Stand at the top of the painting for the full 3-D effect.) As you'll soon see, this palace is wallpapered with Titians, Tintorettos, and Veroneses. Many have the same theme you see here: a doge, in his ermine cape, gold-brocaded robe, and funny one-horned hat with earflaps, kneeling in the presence of saints, gods, or mythological figures.

▶ *Enter the next room.*

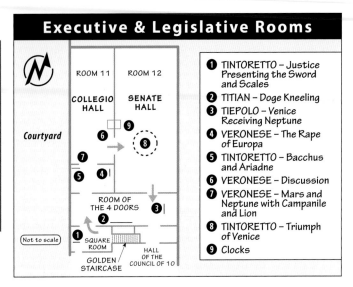

Executive & Legislative Rooms

ROOM 11 ROOM 12

COLLEGIO HALL SENATE HALL

Courtyard

ROOM OF THE 4 DOORS

Not to scale

SQUARE ROOM

GOLDEN STAIRCASE

HALL OF THE COUNCIL OF 10

1 TINTORETTO – Justice Presenting the Sword and Scales
2 TITIAN – Doge Kneeling
3 TIEPOLO – Venice Receiving Neptune
4 VERONESE – The Rape of Europa
5 TINTORETTO – Bacchus and Ariadne
6 VERONESE – Discussion
7 VERONESE – Mars and Neptune with Campanile and Lion
8 TINTORETTO – Triumph of Venice
9 Clocks

Room of the Four Doors (Sala delle Quattro Porte)

This was the central clearinghouse for all the goings-on in the palace. Visitors presented themselves here and were directed to their destination—the courts, councils, or the doge himself. The room was designed by Andrea Palladio, the architect who did the impressive Church of San Giorgio Maggiore, across the Grand Canal from St. Mark's Square. On the intricate stucco ceiling, notice the feet of the women dangling down below the edge (above the windows), extending the illusion.

On the wall to the left of the door you entered from is a painting by Titian, showing a **doge kneeling** with great piety before a woman embodying Faith holding the Cross of Jesus. Notice old Venice in the misty distance under the cross. This is one of many paintings you'll see of doges in uncharacteristically humble poses—paid for, of course, by the doges themselves.

G. B. Tiepolo's well-known *Venice Receiving Neptune* is now displayed on an easel, but it was originally hung on the wall above the windows where they've put a copy. The painting shows Venice as a woman—Venice is always a woman to artists—reclining in luxury,

G. B. Tiepolo's *Venice Receiving Neptune*—the city personified by a sensual woman

dressed in the ermine cape and pearl necklace of a doge's wife (dogaressa). Crude Neptune, enthralled by the First Lady's beauty, arrives bearing a seashell bulging with gold ducats. A bored Venice points and says, "Put it over there with the other stuff."

▶ *Enter the small room with the big fireplace and several paintings.*

Ante-Collegio Hall (Sala dell'Anticollegio)

It took a big title or bribe to get in to see the doge. Once accepted for a visit, you would wait here before you entered, combing your hair, adjusting your robe, popping a breath mint, and preparing the gifts you'd brought. While you cooled your heels and warmed your hands at the elaborate fireplace, you might look at some of the paintings—among the finest in the palace, worthy of any museum in the world.

The Rape of Europa (on the wall opposite the fireplace), by Paolo Veronese, most likely shocked many small-town visitors with its risqué subject matter. Here Zeus, the king of the Greek gods, appears in the form of a bull with a foot fetish, seducing a beautiful earthling while cupids spin playfully overhead.

Tintoretto's ***Bacchus and Ariadne*** (to the right of the fireplace) is another colorful display of Venice's sensual tastes. The God of Wine seeks a threesome, offering a ring to the mortal Ariadne, who's being crowned with stars by Venus, who turns slowly in zero gravity. The ring is the center of a spinning wheel of flesh, with the three arms like spokes.

Veronese's *Rape of Europa* greeted palace visitors with a glimpse into the city's risqué tastes.

▶ *But wait, the doge is ready for us. Let's go in. Enter the next room and approach your imaginary doge.*

Collegio Hall (Sala del Collegio)

Flanked by his cabinet of six advisers—one for each Venetian neighborhood—the doge would sit on the wood-paneled platform at the far end to receive ambassadors, who laid their gifts at his feet and pleaded their countries' cases. All official ceremonies, such as the ratification of treaties, were held here.

At other times, it was the "Oval Office" where the doge and his cabinet (the executive branch) met privately to discuss proposals to give to the legislature, pull files from the cabinets (along the right wall), or rehearse a meeting with the pope. The wooden benches around the sides (where they sat) are original. The clock on the wall is a backward-running 24-hour clock with Roman numerals and a sword for hands.

The ceiling is 24-karat gold, framing paintings by Veronese. These are not frescoes (painting on wet plaster), like those in the Sistine Chapel, but actual canvases painted in Veronese's studio and then placed on the ceiling. Within years, Venice's humidity would have melted frescoes like mascara.

The T-shaped painting of the woman with the spider web (on the ceiling, opposite the big window) represents the Venetian symbol of **Discussion.** You can imagine the webs of truth and lies woven in this room by the doge's scheming advisers. In **Mars and Neptune with Campanile and Lion** (the ceiling painting near the entrance), Veronese presents four symbols of the Republic's strength—military, sea trade, city, and government (plus a cherub about to be circumcised by the Campanile).

▶ *Enter the large Senate Hall.*

Senate Hall (Sala del Senato)

While the doge presided from the stage, senators mounted the podium (middle of the wall with windows) to address their 120 colleagues. The legislators, chaired by the doge, debated and passed laws in this room.

Venice prided itself on its self-rule (independent of popes, kings, and tyrants), with most power placed in the hands of these annually elected men. Which branch of government really ruled? All of them. It was an elaborate system of checks and balances to make sure no one rocked the gondola, no one got too powerful, and the ship of state sailed smoothly ahead.

Tintoretto's large **Triumph of Venice** on the ceiling (central painting, best viewed from the top) shows the city in all its glory. Lady Venice is up in heaven with the Greek gods, while barbaric lesser

Mars and Neptune with Campanile and Lion

Triumph of Venice oversees the Senate.

nations swirl up to give her gifts and tribute. Do you get the feeling the Venetian aristocracy was proud of its city?

On the wall are two large **clocks,** one of which has the signs of the zodiac and phases of the moon. And there's one final oddity in this room, in case you hadn't noticed it yet. In one of the wall paintings (above the entry door), there's actually a doge...not kneeling.

▶ *Exiting the Senate Hall, pass again through the Room of the Four Doors, then around the corner into a hall with a semicircular platform at the far end.*

Hall of the Council of Ten (Sala del Consiglio dei Dieci)

By the 1400s, Venice had a worldwide reputation for swift, harsh, and secret justice. The dreaded Council of Ten—10 judges, plus the doge and his six advisers—met here to dole out punishment to traitors, murderers, and "morals" violators. Note the 17 wood panels where they presided.

This secret council eventually had their own security force of guards, spies, informers, and assassins. It seemed no one was safe from the spying eye of the "Terrible Ten." You could be accused anonymously (by a letter dropped into a Mouth of Truth), swept off the streets, tried, judged, and thrown into the dark dungeons in the palace for the rest of your life without so much as a Miranda warning.

It was in this room that the Council decided who lived or died, and who was decapitated, tortured, or merely thrown in jail. The small, hard-to-find **door** leading off the platform (the fifth panel to the right of center) leads through secret passages to the prisons and torture chambers.

The large, central, oval ceiling painting by Veronese (a copy of the original stolen by Napoleon and still in the Louvre) shows ***Jupiter Descending from Heaven to Strike Down the Vices,*** redundantly informing the accused that justice in Venice was swift and harsh. Though the dreaded Council of Ten was eventually disbanded, today their descendants enforce the dress code at St. Mark's Basilica.

▶ *Pass through the next room, turn right, and head up the stairs to the Armory Museum.*

Armory Museum (L'Armeria)

The aesthetic of killing is beyond me, but I must admit I've never seen a better collection of halberds, falchions, ranseurs, targes, morions,

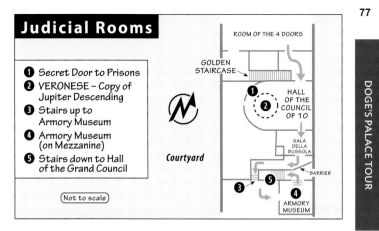

Judicial Rooms

① Secret Door to Prisons
② VERONESE – Copy of Jupiter Descending
③ Stairs up to Armory Museum
④ Armory Museum (on Mezzanine)
⑤ Stairs down to Hall of the Grand Council

ROOM OF THE 4 DOORS
GOLDEN STAIRCASE
HALL OF THE COUNCIL OF 10
SALA DELLA BUSSOLA
BARRIER
ARMORY MUSEUM

Courtyard

(Not to scale)

and brigandines in my life. The weapons in these three rooms make you realize the important role the military played in keeping the East-West trade lines open.

Room 1: In the glass case on the right, you'll see the suit of armor worn by the great Venetian mercenary general, Gattamelata (far right, on horseback), as well as "baby's first armor" (how soon they grow up!). A full suit of armor could weigh 66 pounds. Before gunpowder, crossbows (look up) were made still more lethal by turning a crank on the end to draw the bow with extra force.

Room 2: In the thick of battle, even horses needed helmets. The hefty broadswords were brandished two-handed by the strongest and bravest soldiers who waded into enemy lines. Suspended from the ceiling is a large triangular banner captured from the Ottoman Turks at the Battle of Lepanto (1571).

Room 3: At the far (left) end of the room is a very, very early (17th-century) attempt at a 20-barrel machine gun. On the walls and weapons, the "C-X" insignia means that this was the private stash of the "Council of Ten."

Room 4: In this room, rifles and pistols enter the picture. Don't miss the glass case in the corner, with a tiny crossbow, some torture devices (including an effective-looking thumbscrew), the wooden "devil's box" (a clever item that could fire in four directions at once), and a nasty, two-holed chastity belt. These disheartening "iron breeches" were worn by the devoted wife of the Lord of Padua.

▶ *Exit the Armory Museum. Go downstairs, turn left, and pass through the long hall with a wood-beam ceiling. Now turn right and open your eyes as wide as you can to see the…*

Hall of the Grand Council (Sala del Maggiore Consiglio)

It took a room this size to contain the grandeur of the Most Serene Republic. This huge room (175 by 80 feet) could accommodate up to 2,600 people at one time. The engineering is remarkable. The ceiling is like the deck of a ship—its hull is the rooftop, creating a huge attic above that.

The doge presided from the raised dais, while the nobles—the backbone of the empire—filled the center and lined the long walls. Nobles were generally wealthy men over 25, but the title had less to do with money than with long bloodlines. In theory, the doge, the Senate, and the Council of Ten were all subordinate to the Grand Council of nobles who elected them.

On the wall over the doge's throne is Tintoretto's monsterpiece, ***Paradise,*** the largest oil painting in the world. At 570 square feet, it could be sliced up to wallpaper an apartment with enough left over for placemats.

Christ and Mary are at the top of heaven, surrounded by 500 people. It's rush hour in heaven, and all the good Venetians made it. Tintoretto worked on this in the last years of his long life. On the day it was finished, his daughter died. He got his brush out again and painted her as saint number 501. She's dead-center with the blue skirt,

Tintoretto's *Paradise*—500-plus figures

Siege of Constantinople—Venice triumphs

Hall of the Grand Council

Piazzetta

St. Mark's Basin

SALA DELLO SCRUTINIO

HALL OF THE GRAND COUNCIL

Courtyard

❶ JACOPO TINTORETTO – Paradise

❷ VERONESE – Apotheosis of Venice

❸ Doge Falier (blacked out)

❹ DOMENICO TINTORETTO – Siege of Constantinople

To Prisons & Bridge of Sighs

From Armory Museum

(Not to scale)

hands clasped, getting sucked up to heaven. (At least that's what an Italian tour guide told me.)

Veronese's **The Apotheosis of Venice** (on the ceiling at the Tintoretto end—view it from the top) is a typically unsubtle work showing Lady Venice being crowned a goddess by an angel.

Ringing the hall are portraits, in chronological order, of the first 76 doges. The one at the far end that's blacked out is the notorious **Doge Marin Falier,** who opposed the will of the Grand Council in 1355. He was tried for treason, beheaded, and airbrushed from history.

Along the entire wall to the right of Paradise, the **Siege of Constantinople** (by Tintoretto's son, Domenico) shows Venice's greatest military (if not moral) victory, the conquest of the fellow-Christian city of Constantinople during the Fourth Crusade (see sidebar on page 53). The sneaky Venetians (in the fifth painting) attacked the mighty city from the water. They cozied their galleys right up to the dock and scooted across the masts to the city walls. The gates open, the Byzantine emperor parades out to surrender, and tiny Doge Dandolo says, "Let's go in and steal some bronze horses."

But soon Venice would begin its long slide into historical oblivion. The rising Ottoman Turks gobbled up Venice's trading outposts.

New trade routes to the East and America broke Venice's monopoly on trade. The once-mighty empire was reduced to little more than the city itself, a tourist town with a reputation for decadence. Finally, in 1797, the French general Napoleon marched into town shouting *"Liberté, egalité, fraternité."* The Most Serene Republic was overthrown, and the last doge was deposed in the name of modern democracy.

▶ *Consider reading about the prisons here in the Grand Council Hall, where there are more benches and fewer rats.*

To reach the prisons, exit the Grand Hall by squeezing through the door to the left of Tintoretto's monsterpiece. Follow signs for Prigioni/Ponte dei Sospiri, *passing through several rooms. In a room adjoining Room 31, you'll find a narrow staircase going down, following signs to the prisons. (Don't miss it, or you'll miss the prisons altogether and end up at the bookshop near the exit.) Then cross the covered Bridge of Sighs over the canal to the prisons. Start your visit in the cells to your left.*

Prisons

The palace had its own dungeons. In the privacy of his own home, a doge could oversee the sentencing, torturing, and jailing of political opponents. By the 1500s, the dungeons were full of political prisoners, so new prisons were built across the canal connected with a covered bridge.

Circle the cells. Medieval justice was harsh. The cells consisted of cold stone with heavily barred windows, a wooden plank for a bed, a shelf, and a bucket. (My question: What did they put on the shelf?) You can feel the cold and damp. Notice the carvings made by prisoners—from olden days up until 1930—on some of the stone windowsills of the cells, especially in the far corner of the building.

Explore the rest of the prisons. You can descend lower to the notorious cells known as "the wells"—so-called because they were deep, wet, and cramped. Or stay on this floor, where there's a room displaying ceramic shards found in archaeological digs. Adjoining that are more cells, including the farthest cell, where you can see the bored prisoners' compelling and sometimes artistic graffiti. The singing gondoliers outside are a reminder of how tantalizingly close these pitiful prisoners were to one of the world's finest cities.

▶ *Wherever you roam, you'll end up where you entered. Now go back across the...*

Bridge of Sighs

According to romantic legend, criminals were tried and sentenced in the palace, then marched across the canal here to the dark prisons. On this bridge, they got one last look at Venice. They gazed out at the sky, the water, and the beautiful buildings.

▶ *As you cross the Bridge of Sighs, pause to look through the marble-trellised windows at all of the tourists and the heavenly Church of San Giorgio Maggiore. Heave one last sigh and leave the palace.*

It's a romantic scene today, but the "sighs" from this bridge once came from condemned prisoners.

Frari Church Tour

Basilica di Santa Maria Gloriosa dei Frari

For me, this church offers the best art-appreciation experience in Venice, because so much of its great art is in situ—right where it was designed to be seen, rather than hanging in museums.

The church was built (and consecrated in 1492) by the Franciscan order. They were inspired by St. Francis of Assisi (c. 1182-1226), who dedicated himself to a nonmaterialistic lifestyle. The spirit of St. Francis of Assisi warms both the church of his "brothers" (*frari*) and the art that decorates it. The Franciscan love of all of creation—Nature and Man—later inspired Renaissance painters to capture the beauty of the physical world and human emotions, showing worshippers the glory of God in human terms.

ORIENTATION

Cost: €3.

Hours: Mon-Sat 9:00-18:00, Sun 13:00-18:00.

Information: Tel. 041-272-8618, www.basilicadeifrari.it.

Dress Code: Modest dress is recommended.

Getting There: It's near the San Tomà vaporetto and *traghetto* stops. From the dock, follow signs to *Scuola Grande di San Rocco*. For a pleasant stroll from the Rialto Bridge, ❂ take the Rialto to Frari Church Walk.

Tours: Rent an audioguide for €2, or 🎧 download this chapter as a free Rick Steves audio tour (see page 193).

Length of This Tour: Allow one hour.

Eating: The church square is ringed with small, simple, reasonably priced cafés.

Nearby: For efficient sightseeing, combine your visit with the nearby Scuola San Rocco and the Ca' Rezzonico, a seven-minute walk away.

Starring: Titian, Giovanni Bellini, Paolo Veneziano, and Donatello.

THE TOUR BEGINS

▶ *Enter the church, let your eyes adjust, and stand just inside the door with a good view down the long nave toward the altar.*

Frari Church

To Scuola
San Rocco

Campo San Rocco

To
Accademia

ALTAR

Not to scale

S A C R I S T Y

TRANSEPT

CHAPTER
HOUSE

CHOIR

❶ View of Church Interior
& Choir

❷ TITIAN – Assumption of
the Virgin

❸ Tomb of Doge Foscari

❹ DONATELLO – Statue of
John the Baptist

❺ GIO. BELLINI – Madonna and
Child with Saints and Angels

❻ VENEZIANO – Madonna and
Child with Doge Francesco
Dandolo

❼ Tomb of Titian

❽ Canova Monument

❾ TITIAN – Madonna of
Ca' Pesaro

N
A
V
E

Campo
dei
Frari

To
Rialto

TOUR BEGINS

TICKETS

ENTRY

❶ Church Interior and Choir (1250-1443)

The simple, spacious (110-yard-long), well-lit Gothic church—with rough wood crossbeams and a red-and-white color scheme—is truly a remarkable sight in a city otherwise crammed with exotic froufrou. Because Venice's spongy ground could never support a real stone Gothic church (such as those you'd find in France), the Frari is made of light and flexible brick. Traditionally, churches in Venice were cross-shaped, but this T-shaped footprint featured a long, lofty nave—flooded with light and suited to large gatherings—where common people heard sermons.

The wooden choir area in the center of the nave allowed friars to hold smaller, more intimate services. From the early 16th century, as worshippers entered the church and looked down the long nave to the altar, they were greeted by Titian's glorious painted altarpiece—then, as now, framed by the arch of the choir entrance.

Walk prayerfully toward the Titian, stopping in the gorgeously carved 1480s choir. Notice the fine inlay above the chairs, showing the Renaissance enthusiasm for Florentine-style depth and perspective.

▶ *Approach Titian's heavenly vision.*

❷ Titian (Tiziano Vecellio)—*The Assumption of the Virgin* (1516-1518)

Glowing red and gold like a stained-glass window, this altarpiece sets the tone of exuberant beauty found in this otherwise sparse church. At the end of her life (though looking 17 here), Mary was miraculously "assumed" into heaven. As cherubs lift her up to meet a Jupiter-like God, the stunned apostles on earth reach up to touch the floating bubble of light.

Look around. The church is littered with chapels and tombs "made possible by the generous financial support" of rich people who donated to the Franciscans for the good of their souls (and usually for tomb-topping statues of themselves, as well).

For the altar, they hired the new whiz artist, Titian, to create a dramatic painting. Unveiled in 1518, the work scandalized a Venice accustomed to simpler, more contemplative church art. The rich colors, twisting poses, and mix of saccharine angels with blue-collar apostles were unheard of. Most striking, this Virgin is fully human, not a stiff icon on a throne. The Franciscans thought this Mary aroused excitement rather than spirituality. They agreed to pay Titian only after the Holy Roman Emperor offered to buy the altar if they refused.

In a burst of youthful innovation, Titian (1488-1576) had rewritten the formula for church art, hinting at changes to come with the Mannerist and Baroque styles. He energized the scene with a complex composition, overlapping a circle (Mary's bubble) and a triangle (draw a line from the apostle reaching up to Mary's face and down the other side) on three horizontal levels (God in heaven, Man on earth, Mary in between). Together, these elements draw our eyes from the swirl of arms and legs to the painting's focus—the radiant face of a triumphant Mary, "assumed body and soul into heaven."

Titian's *Assumption*—as she rises to heaven, Mary radiates spirituality through physical beauty

▶ *Flanking the painting are marble tombs lining the walls. On the wall to the right of the altar is the...*

❸ Tomb of Doge Foscari (15th Century)

This heavy, ornate tomb marks the peak of Venice's worldly power. Doge Francesco Foscari (1373-1457) assumed control of the city's powerful seafaring empire and then tried to expand it onto the mainland, battling Milan in a 31-year war of attrition that swept through northern Italy. Meanwhile, on the unprotected eastern front, the Ottomans took Constantinople (1453) and scuttled Venice's trade. Venice's long slide into historical oblivion had begun. Financially drained city fathers forced Foscari to resign, turn in his funny hat, and hand over the keys to the Doge's Palace.

▶ *In the first chapel to the right of the altar, you'll find...*

❹ Donatello—*Statue of John the Baptist* (1438)

In the center of the altarpiece, the cockeyed prophet of the desert—emaciated from his breakfast of bugs 'n' honey and dressed in animal skins—freezes mid-rant when he spies something in the distance. His jaw goes slack, and he twists his face and raises his hand to announce the coming of...the Renaissance.

Florentine expatriates living in Venice commissioned Donatello to make this wooden statue, and it reflects their tastes. The Renaissance began in the Florence of the 1400s, where Donatello (1386-1466) created realistic statues with a full range of human emotions. This warts-and-all John the Baptist is harshly realistic, with muted colors. By contrast, Venetian art is generally soft-focus and beautiful, with bright colors.

Donatello's bold *John the Baptist* (center)   Bellini's *Madonna* in an illusory niche

▶ *Enter the sacristy through the door at the far end of the right transept. You'll bump into an elaborate altar crammed with reliquaries. Opposite that (near the entrance door) is a clock, intricately carved from a single piece of wood. At the far end of the room, you'll find Bellini's glowing altarpiece.*

❺ Giovanni Bellini—*Madonna and Child with Saints and Angels* (1488)

The Pesaro family, who negotiated an acceptable price and place for their family tomb, funded this delightful chapel dominated by a Bellini masterpiece.

Mary sits on a throne under a half-dome, propping up Baby Jesus (who's just learning to stand), flanked by saints and serenaded by musician angels. Giovanni Bellini (c. 1430-1516), the father of the Venetian Renaissance, painted fake columns and a dome to match the real ones in the gold frame, making the painting seem to be an extension of the room. He completes the illusion with glimpses of open sky in the background. Next, he fills the artificial niches with symmetrically posed, thoughtful saints—left to right, find Saints Nicholas, Peter, Mark, and Sean Connery (Benedict).

Bellini combined the meditative poses of the Venetian Byzantine tradition with Renaissance improvements in modern art. He made the transition from painting with medieval tempera (egg yolk-based) to painting in oil (pigments dissolved in vegetable oil). Oils allowed a subtler treatment of colors because artists could apply them in successive layers. And because darker colors aren't so muddy when painted in oil, they "pop," effectively giving the artist a brighter palette.

Bellini virtually invented the formula (later to be broken by his precocious pupil, Titian) for Venetian altarpieces. This type of holy conversation (*Sacra Conversazione*) between saints and Mary can also be seen in Venice's Accademia and Church of San Zaccaria.

Renaissance humanism demanded Madonnas and saints that were accessible and human. Bellini delivers, but places them in a physical setting so beautiful that it creates its own mood of serene holiness. The scene is lit from the left, but nothing casts a harsh shadow—Mary and the babe are enveloped in a glowing aura of reflected light from the golden dome. The beauty is in the details, from the writing in the dome, to the red brocade backdrop, to the swirls in the marble steps, to the angels' dimpled legs.

Veneziano's *Madonna*—solemn, icon-like faces and a neutral background show Byzantine roots

▶ *In the adjoining room, find a painting in the shape of a Gothic arch.*

❻ Paolo Veneziano—*Madonna and Child with Doge Francesco Dandolo* (c. 1339)

Bellini's Byzantine roots can be traced to Paolo Veneziano (literally, "Paul the Venetian"), the first "name" artist in Venice, who helped shape the distinctive painting style of his city. Veneziano paints Byzantine icons, then sets them in motion. Baby Jesus turns to greet a kneeling Doge Dandolo, while Mary turns to acknowledge the doge's wife. None other than St. Francis presents "Francis" (Francesco) Dandolo to the Madonna. Both he and St. Elizabeth (on the right) bend at the waist and gesture as naturally as 14th-century icons can.

▶ *Return to the nave and head left, back toward the main entrance. Turn around and face the altar. In the second bay on your right is the...*

❼ Tomb of Titian (1852)

The enormous carved marble monument is labeled "Titiano Ferdinandus MDCCCLII." The tomb celebrates both the man and his famous paintings (depicted in the background reliefs).

Titian (c. 1488/90-1576) sits center stage, with a beard and crown of laurels. Titian was the greatest Venetian painter, excelling equally in inspirational altarpieces, realistic portraits, joyous mythological scenes, and erotic female nudes.

As a young man, he studied as a mosaic-maker and then a painter under Giovanni Bellini and Giorgione. Soon he established his own bold style, which featured teenage Madonnas, like the Frari altarpiece (see a relief of *The Assumption* behind Titian). He became wealthy and famous, traveling Europe to paint stately portraits of kings and nobles, and colorful, sexy works for their bedrooms. But he always returned to his beloved Venice (see winged lion on top)...and favorite Frari Church.

In his old age, Titian painted dark, tragic masterpieces. His *Pietà* (see relief in upper left) was intended for his tomb but ended up in the Accademia (✪ see page 133). Nearing 90, he labored to finish the *Pietà* as the plague enveloped Venice. One in four people died, including Titian's son. Heartbroken, Titian died soon afterward. The cause of death was probably the plague, although his death was officially chalked up to influenza to keep his body from being burned—a requirement for plague victims. His tomb was built three centuries later to remember and honor this great Venetian.

▶ *On the opposite side of the nave is the pyramid-shaped...*

❽ Canova Monument (1827)

Antonio Canova (1757-1822, see his portrait above the door) was Venice's greatest sculptor. He created gleaming white, highly polished statues of beautiful Greek gods and goddesses in the Neoclassical style. (✪ See several of his works at the Correr Museum, page 127.)

The pyramid shape is timeless, suggesting pharaohs' tombs and

Titian's tomb—Venice's greatest painter

Canova Monument—its greatest sculptor

the Christian Trinity. Mourners, bent over with grief, shuffle up to pay homage to the master artist. Even the winged lion is choked up.

Follow me here. Canova himself designed this pyramid-shaped tomb, not for his own use, but as the tomb of an artist he greatly admired: Titian. But the Frari picked another design for Titian's tomb, so Canova used the pyramid for an Austrian princess in Vienna. After his death, Canova's pupils copied the design here to honor their master. In fact, Canova isn't buried here—he lies in southern Italy. But inside the tomb's open door, you can (barely) see an urn, which contains his heart.

▶ *Head back toward the altar. Halfway up the left wall is...*

❾ Titian—*Madonna of Ca' Pesaro* (1519-1526)

Titian's second altarpiece for the Frari Church displays all his many skills. Following his teacher Bellini, he puts Mary (seated) and baby (standing) on a throne, surrounded by saints having a holy conversation. And, like Bellini, he paints fake columns that echo the church's real ones.

But wait. Mary is off-center, Titian's idealized saints mingle with Venetians sporting five o'clock shadows, and the stairs run diagonally away from us. Mary sits not on a throne, but on a pedestal. Baby Jesus is restless. The precious keys of St. Peter seem to dangle unnoticed. These things upset traditional Renaissance symmetry, but they turn a group of figures into a true scene. St. Peter (center, in blue and gold, with book) looks down at Jacopo Pesaro, who kneels to thank the Virgin for his recent naval victory over the Ottomans (1502). A flag-carrying lieutenant drags in a turbaned captive. Meanwhile, St. Francis talks to Baby Jesus while gesturing down to more members of the Pesaro family. The little guy looking out at us (lower right) is the Pesaro descendant who administered the trust fund to keep prayers coming for his dead uncle.

Titian combines opposites: a soft-focus Madonna with photo-realist portraits, chubby winged angels with a Muslim prisoner, and a Christian cross with a battle flag. In keeping with the spirit of St. Francis' humanism, Titian lets mere mortals mingle with saints. And we're right there with them.

▶ *While this church is a great example of art in situ, in a sense, all of Venice is art in situ. Explore some back lanes and lonely canals here on the meditative side of town.*

Madonna of Ca' Pesaro—saints mingle with Venetians, making the heavenly seem real

St. Mark's to Rialto Loop Walk

Two rights and a left (simple!) can get you from St. Mark's Square to the Rialto Bridge via a completely different route from the one most tourists take. Along the way, take in some lesser sights and appreciate the reality of Venice today.

Venice's population is half what it was just 30 years ago. Sad, yes, but imagine raising a family here: Apartments are small, high up, and expensive. Home-improvement projects involve miles of red tape. Running a simple errand can mean crossing arched bridges while pushing a child in a stroller and carrying a day's worth of groceries.

On the other hand, those who stay couldn't think of living anywhere else. This walk may help you understand why.

ORIENTATION

Length of This Walk: Allow one hour for a leisurely walk.
San Moisè Church: Free, Mon-Sat 9:30-12:30 & 15:30-18:30, tel. 041-296-0630.
La Fenice Opera House: €10 for dry 45-minute audioguide tour, generally open daily 9:30-18:00, theater box office open daily 10:00-17:00, box office tel. 041-2424, www.teatrolafenice.it.
Rialto Market: The souvenir stalls are open daily; the produce market is closed on Sunday; and the fish market is closed on Sunday and Monday. The market is lively only in the morning.

THE WALK BEGINS

▶ *From St. Mark's Square, walk to the waterfront and turn right. You're walking on recently raised Venice—in 2006, the stones were taken up and six inches of extra sand put down, to minimize flooding. Continue along the water toward the white TI pavilion.*

Waterfront

Along the waterfront, you'll see the various boats that ply Venice's waters. Hiring a gondola here is often more expensive than elsewhere in Venice. Classic wooden motorboats operating as water taxis are pricey (about €60 from here to the train station), but they are a classy splurge if you split the fare with others. Hotel shuttle boats bring guests here from distant, $700-a-night hotels.

Run the gauntlet of souvenir stands to the entrance to the Giardinetti Reali (Royal Gardens, once the site of a huge grain-storage depot that was destroyed by Napoleon). The grounds (with ample benches) offer some precious greenery in a city built of stone on mud. After the park entrance, the walkway runs right into the TI, in a cute 18th-century former coffeehouse pavilion. Go around the left side of the TI pavilion and—from atop the bridge—look across the mouth of the Grand Canal to view the big dome of La Salute Church. The guy balancing a bronze ball on one foot is on top of the old Customs House, which now houses the Punta della Dogana contemporary art museum.

▶ *Twelve steps down and 20 yards ahead on the right is...*

St. Mark's to Rialto Loop Walk

① Harry's American Bar
② San Moisè Church
③ La Fenice Opera House
④ Ponte de la Verona
⑤ Campo Manin
⑥ Scala Contarini del Bovolo
⑦ Teatro Goldoni
⑧ Rialto Bridge
⑨ Campo San Bartolomeo
⑩ Casino
⑪ Clock Tower

The waterfront by St. Mark's Square

Harry's Bar—overpriced "celebrity" haunt

❶ Harry's American Bar

Hemingway put this bar on the map by making it his hangout in the late 1940s. If George and Amal are in town, this is where they'll be. If they're not, you'll see plenty of dressed-up Americans looking around for celebrities. The discreet (and overpriced) restaurant upstairs is where the glitterati hang out. The street-level bar is for gawkers. If you wear something a bit fancy (or artsy bohemian), you can pull up a stool at the tiny bar by the entrance and pay too much for a Bellini (prosecco and peach puree), which was invented right here.

▶ *Head inland down Calle Vallaresso, one of Venice's most exclusive streets, past fancy boutiques such as Tiffany, Brunello Cucinelli, and Roberto Cavalli. At the T intersection, turn left and head west on Salizada San Moisè (which becomes Calle Larga XXII Marzo). Continue to the first bridge and a square dominated by the fancy facade of a church. Climb the bridge, and against a soundtrack of tourists negotiating with hustling gondoliers, look back at the ornate...*

❷ San Moisè Church

This is the parish church for St Mark's; because of tourist crowds at the basilica, this is where the community used to worship, but it no longer offers Mass. While it's one of Venice's oldest churches, dating from the 10th century (note the old tower on the right), its busy facade is 17th-century Baroque. The big shot who funded the project has his bust in the center of the facade, while Moses (Moisè) caps it.

Inside, the altarpiece depicts Mount Sinai, with Moses (kneeling) receiving the two tablets with the Ten Commandments. The alcove to the left of the altar has Tintoretto's 16th-century *Christ Washing the Disciples' Feet*.

The modern building nearby is the ritzy, five-star Bauer Hotel, originally an 18th-century palace. In the 1940s, the owners added this Fascist-deco wing, defying Italian historical-preservation codes. Its facade still gives locals the Mussolini-creeps. You can take a few minutes to wander through the hotel for a James Bond-meets-Mussolini architectural experience.

▶ *Continue over the bridge, down Calle Larga XXII Marzo, a big street that seems too wide and large for Venice. It was created during the 19th century by filling in a canal. You can make out the outline of the sidewalks that once flanked the now-gone canal. Pass by the Vivaldi lookalikes selling concert tickets and (mostly Senegalese) immigrants illegally selling knockoffs of Prada bags.*

Halfway down the street, after passing the grand Borsa, turn right on tiny Calle del Sartor da Veste. Go straight, crossing a bridge. At the next square, you'll find…

❸ La Fenice Opera House (Gran Teatro alla Fenice)

Venice's famed opera house, completed in 1792 (read the MDCCXCII on the facade), was started as a business venture by a group of nobles who recognized that Venice was short on entertainment opportunities for the well-heeled set.

La Fenice was reduced to a hollowed-out shell by a disastrous fire in 1996. After a vigorous restoration campaign, "The Phoenix"—true to its name—has risen again from the ashes. La Fenice resumed opera productions in 2004, opening with *La Traviata*. The theater is usually open daily to the public.

San Moisè Church and Bauer Hotel

"The Phoenix," a classic opera house

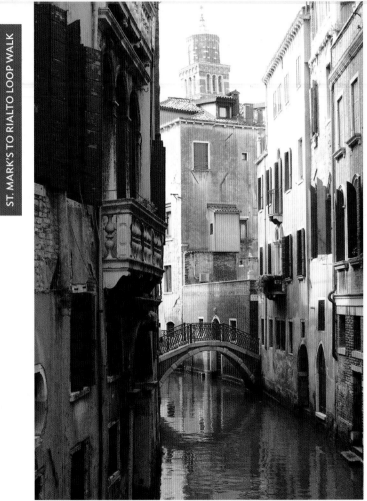

View from Ponte de la Verona—a slice of everyday life that's both charming and crumbling

Venice is one of the cradles of the multimedia art form known as opera. Some of the great operas were first performed here in this luxurious setting. Verdi's *Rigoletto* (1851) and *La Traviata* (1853) were actually commissioned by La Fenice. The man who put words to some of Mozart's opera tunes was a Venetian, Lorenzo da Ponte, who drew inspiration from the city's libertine ways and joie de vivre. In recent years, La Fenice's musical standing was overshadowed by its reputation as a place for the wealthy to parade in furs and jewels.

▶ *Passing La Fenice, continue north along the same street (though its name is now Calle de la Verona), to a small bridge over a quiet canal.*

❹ Ponte de la Verona

Pause atop this bridge, where reflections can make you wonder which end is up. Looking above you, see bridges of stone propping up leaning buildings, and the view of the "Leaning Tower" of San Stefano.

People actually live in Venice. Notice their rooftop gardens, their laundry, their plumbing, electricity lines snaking into their apartments, and the rusted iron bars and bolts that hold their crumbling homes together. On one building, find centuries-old relief carvings—a bearded face and a panel of an eagle with its prey. People once swam freely in the canals. Find the sign that reads *Divieto di Nuoto* ("swimming not allowed").

You may see some private boats. Italian law stipulates that a luxury tax is levied on all boats—except in Venice, where they're considered a necessity. Calling a taxi? A boat comes. Going to the hospital to have a baby? Take an ambulance boat. Garbage day? You put your bag on the canal edge, and a garbage boat mashes it and takes it away. While many Venetians own (and love) their own boats, parking is a huge problem. If you take your boat to run errands, you either know a friend nearby with a grandfathered parking space, or your partner has to "circle the block" while you shop.

While many Venetians own a car for driving on the isle of Lido or the mainland, they admit, "We're not very much beloved on the road."

▶ *Continue north. At the T intersection, turn right on Calle de la Mandola. You'll cross over a bridge into a spacious square dominated by a statue and an out-of-place modern building.*

❺ Campo Manin

The centerpiece of the square is a statue of Daniele Manin (1804-1857), one of a group of patriotic visionaries who foresaw the unification of Italy (the Risorgimento) 20 years before it happened. The statue faces the red house Manin lived in.

▶ *Scala Contarini del Bovolo is a block south of here, with yellow signs pointing the way. Facing the Manin statue, turn right and exit the square down an alley. Turn left with the street, then immediately follow yellow signs to the left, then immediately to the right, into a courtyard with one of Venice's hidden treasures...*

❻ Scala Contarini del Bovolo

The Scala is a cylindrical brick tower with five floors of spiral staircases faced with white marble banisters (probably closed for renovation during your visit).

Built in 1499, it was the external staircase of a palace (external stairs saved interior space for rooms). Architecture buffs admire the successful blend of a Gothic building with a Renaissance staircase.

If the tower is open, you can pay a small fee to wind your way up the "snail shell" (*bovolo* in the local dialect). It's 113 steps to the top, where you're rewarded with views of the Venetian skyline.

▶ *Unwind and return to the Manin statue. Continue east, circling around the right side of the big Cassa di Risparmio bank, marveling at its Modernist ugliness. At Campo San Luca, walk halfway through the square, then turn left (north) on Calle del Forno. Note the 24-hour pharmacy vending machine (on the right) that dispenses shower gel, Band-Aids, bug repellant, toothbrushes, condoms, and other after-hours*

Daniele Manin, 19th-century patriot

The photogenic Scala Contarini del Bovolo

necessities. Heading north, glance 20 yards down the street to the right at the flag-bedecked...

❼ Teatro Goldoni

Though this theater dates from the 1930s, there's been a theater here since the 1500s, when Venice was at the forefront of secular entertainment. Many of Carlo Goldoni's (1707-1793) groundbreaking comedies—featuring real-life situations of the new middle class—got their first performances here. Today, Teatro Goldoni is still a working theater of mainly Italian productions.

▶ *Continue north on Calle del Forno. You're very close to the Grand Canal. Keep going north, angling to the right through the small square (Corte del Teatro), then left down a teeny-tiny alleyway. Pop! You emerge on the Grand Canal, about 150 yards downstream from the...*

❽ Rialto Bridge

Of Venice's more than 400 bridges, only four cross the Grand Canal. Rialto was the first among these four.

The original Rialto Bridge, dating from 1180, was a platform supported by boats tied together. It linked the political side (Palazzo Ducale) of Venice with the economic center (Rialto). Rialto, which

The Rialto Bridge, lined with shops, is the geographic "heart" of fish-shaped Venice.

takes its name from *riva alto* (high bank), was one of the earliest Venetian settlements. When Venice was Europe's economic super-power, this was where bankers, brokers, and merchants conducted their daily business.

Rialto Bridge II was a 13th-century wooden drawbridge. It was replaced in 1588 by the current structure, with its bold single arch (spanning 160 feet) and arcades on top designed to strengthen the stone span. Its immense foundations stretch 650 feet on either side. Heavy buildings were then built atop the foundations to hold every-thing in place. The Rialto remained the only bridge crossing the Grand Canal until 1854.

Marking the geographical center of Venice (midway down the Grand Canal), the Rialto is the most sensible location for retail shops. The government built it with the (accurate) expectation that it'd soon pay for itself with rent from the shops built into it. Like the (older) Ponte Vecchio in Florence, the Rialto was originally lined with luxury gold-and-jewelry shops. The bridge is cleverly designed to generate maximum rent: three lanes, two rows of twelve shops each, with a warehouse area above each shop under the lead-and-timber roof.

Reliefs of the Venetian Republic's main mascots, St. Mark and St. Theodore, crown the arch. Barges and vaporetti run the busy water-ways below, and merchants vie for tourists' attention on top.

The Rialto has long been a symbol of Venice. Aristocratic inhabit-ants built magnificent palaces just to be near it. The poetic Lord Byron swam to it all the way from Lido Island. And thousands of marriage proposals have been sealed right here, with a kiss, as the moon floated over La Serenissima.

▶ *From here, you could cross the bridge to check out the fish-and-produce market. Or continue even farther along my* ✪ *Rialto to Frari Church Walk (the next chapter). But this walk returns along the main tourist route to St. Mark's Square. From the base of the Rialto Bridge (on the San Marco side), go 100 yards directly to...*

❾ Campo San Bartolomeo

This square is one of the city's main crossroads. Locals routinely meet at the statue of playwright Carlo Goldoni. The pharmacy on this square (marked by a green cross) keeps an electronic counter in its window, ticking down the population of Venice as it shrinks.

Playwright Carlo Goldoni

Stucco work adorns this casino.

▶ *Head to the right 100 yards, down Via 2 Aprile, setting your sights on the green-and-red umbrellas on the corner. They mark a stretch of town once famous for selling umbrellas and handbags. From there, turn left and follow the crowds 100 yards more along Marzaria San Salvador, a.k.a. the...*

Mercerie

The high-rent Mercerie (or "Marzarie," in Venetian dialect) is a string of connecting streets lined mostly with tacky tourist shops. Much of the "Venetian" glass displayed here is actually made in China (always look for the Murano symbol). The Caputo shop—behind the Rolex shop, down an alley and on the left—is handy for phone and camera needs.

▶ *When you get to the yellow two-way arrow "directing" you to San Marco, head right and then follow the flow left another 100 yards until you reach a bridge, which makes for a fun gondola viewing perch. At the top of the bridge, belly up to the railing on the left. Above the arcade on your left is the fancy little iron balcony of the city's best-preserved...*

❿ Casino

While humble from the outside, the interior is a great example of a classic Venetian space. If the windows are open, spy the lacy pastel and stucco ceilings inside. Though only a few of Venice's casinos still exist, the city once had several hundred of these "little houses"—city-center retreats for the palazzo-dwelling set. For many patricians, they served as 17th-century man caves, used for entertaining, gambling, and/or intimate encounters. For well-to-do women, casinos provided a different kind of escape: Inspired by Madame de Pompadour (Louis

XV's mistress), ladies would hold court with writers, artists, and avant-garde types.

▶ *Cross the bridge and continue straight for 100 yards along Marzaria San Zulian. On the way, notice the metal two-foot-high flood-barrier braces at shop doors—and how merchandise is elevated in anticipation of high water (local insurance doesn't cover floods).*

When you hit the next schizophrenic Per S. Marco arrow (in front of the church), go right a few steps, then left onto Marzaria dell'Orologio, a street named for where you're heading: the Clock Tower. The Renaissance ⓫ **Clock Tower** was built when it was considered important that cities have a proper main gate with a grand clock. Pass through "Venice's front door" and back into its grand courtyard—St. Mark's Square.

Rialto to Frari Church Walk

Cross the Rialto Bridge, and dive headlong into Venice's thriving market area. Smell the fresh-caught fish, ogle the produce, and rub shoulders with Venetian shoppers following the same rhythm of life that's gone on here for generations. Home to a number of colorful *cicchetti* pubs, this area is a great place for lunch. From the market, we'll continue on another 20 minutes through the less-touristed San Polo neighborhood—a place where "real" Venetians live. We'll pass workaday stores, neighborhood squares, and one of Venice's best mask shops. Finally, we'll spill out at Tintoretto's Scuola San Rocco and the art-filled Frari Church.

ORIENTATION

Length of This Walk: Allow a leisurely hour.

When to Go: The markets are lively only in the morning. The produce market is closed on Sunday, and the fish market is closed on Sunday and Monday.

Church of San Polo: €3, Mon-Sat 10:30-16:30, closed Sun.

Tragicomica Mask Shop: Daily 10:00-19:00, on Calle dei Nomboli at #2800, tel. 041-721-102, www.tragicomica.it. The owners are generally happy to show their workshop on weekdays to customers who buy a mask, though it's best to make a reservation.

Eateries: Many pubs and restaurants in the Rialto area are recommended in the Eating chapter.

THE WALK BEGINS

▶ *From the top of the Rialto Bridge, walk down the bridge (heading away from the St. Mark's side) and about 50 yards onward until you see an old square on your right. Go to its fountain.*

❶ Campo San Giacomo

The square looks like it did in the 16th century. This High Renaissance square was built in 1520—or "MDXX," as it says on the arcade—after a fire devastated the area. The church, which escaped the fire, has one of the oldest facades in town, with a clock that predates minute hands.

Notice that the square slopes toward the center. Originally, rainwater flowed to the center, and filtered down through limestone, where it was collected in an underground cistern. Several thousand cisterns like this provided the city with its drinking water up until 1886, when an aqueduct was built (paralleling the railroad bridge) to bring in water from nearby mountains.

Back when the Rialto Bridge was a drawbridge (until the 1590s), big ships would dock here to unload their spices, oil, wine, and jewels. The line of buildings between Campo San Giacomo and the canal was once a strip of banks—the Bancogiro. Today it's a line of popular eateries (described on page 165). Behind today's trashy jewelry stands are real jewelry shops, which have thrived here for more than 500 years.

Opposite the church, find the granite hunchback supporting steps leading to a column. Back when this prosperous neighborhood was Europe's "Wall Street," the column was its *"Wall Street Journal."* A man climbed the stair each noon, stood atop the column, and read aloud the daily news from the doge: which ships had docked, which foreign ambassadors were in town, the price of pepper, and so on.

Walk along the left side of the church and turn left, to the canal's edge. Look back at the large white building behind the church (the city's fiscal administration building). Notice how it tilts out, probably because the bridge's huge foundation is compressing the mud beneath it.

Now turn right and walk along the canal to a little canalside dead-end that's as close as you can get to the Rialto Bridge. Take in the great view of the bridge. The former post office (directly across from you) was originally the German merchants' hall (see the seal). It's been reincarnated as a Benetton-owned shopping center.

You're standing under a former prison. Study the iron grills over the windows. Notice the interlocking pipes with alternating joints—you couldn't cut just one and escape.

▶ *From the prison, walk back along the canal, proceed through the triple archway, cross the square, and enter the square named Casaria (for the historic cheese market). Today, this is Venice's...*

❷ Produce Market (Erberia)

Colorful stalls offer fresh fruit and vegetables, some quite exotic. Nothing is grown on the island of Venice, so everything is shipped in daily from the mainland. The Rialto Mercato vaporetto stop is a convenient place for boats to unload their wares, here in the heart of

Cross the Rialto Brigde into less-touristed Venice.   Campo San Giacomo, near the Rialto Market

Rialto to Frari Church Walk

Campo Nazario Sauro

RUGA BELLA

SANTA CROCE

Campiello Strope

CORTE DEL PRETI

C. DE LE OCHE
C. OCHE
CORTE DEI TENTOR
CORTE MARIANI

Campo San Boldo

C. D. MODENA

Campo Santa Maria Mater Domini

C. LONGA

C. DE L'AGNELLO

FOND. RIO MARIN

C. VENZATO

CALLE DE L'OGIO

C. SAN ZUANE

Rio de San Giacomo

R. TERA PRIMO ASTORI

C. D. CRISTO

C. BERNARDO

Rio de la Madoneta

CORTE VITALBA

CALLE DE L'OGIO

CALLE ZANE

C. TABACCO
C. DE LA VIDA

Rio de S. Agostin

C. DE CA' CORNER

To Piazzale Roma

RIO TERA SAN TOMA

Campo San Stin

C. DE CA' DONA
C. SORANZO

FOND. CONTARINI

Rio de S. Stin

Rio de San Polo

Campo San Polo

5

CALLE CAVALLI

SAN ROCCO

F. DEI FRARI

FRARI

RIO TERA

SAN POLO

6

C. DE MADONET

Campo San Rocco

Campo dei Frari

C. 2 D. SAONERI

CALLE D. SAONERI

MADONA

SCUOLA SAN ROCCO

C. DE LA PASSION

C. LARGA

C. DEL VOLTI

NOMBOLI

R. PISANI

PALAZZO BERNARDO

PALAZZO CAPPELLO-LAYARD

WALK ENDS

C. CALIPOLI

GOZZI

F. DONA ONESTA
C. DEL CRISTO

Campo San Tomà

C. DEL TRAGHETO

C. CENTANI

7

PALAZZO BARBARIGO

Grand

S. PANTALON

CROSERA

ONESTA

SAN TOMÀ

CAMPANIEL

PALAZZO GIUSTINIANI

T

Sant'Angelo

A V

C. DE LA SAONERIA

C. DONA ONESTA

C. MARCONA

PALAZZO BALBI

V

San Tomà

PALAZZO MOCENIGO

PALAZZO CORNER-SPINELLI

To Accademia

C. LARGA FOSCARI

To Ferrovia
(Train Station)

SAN
CASSIAN

**FISH
MARKET**

Campo
de la
Pescaria

Campo
Cassian

C. BECARIE

Campo
de le
Becarie

Rialto
Mercato

**PRODUCE
MARKET**

SAN
GIACOMO
DE RIALTO

SAN POLO

Campo
Rialto
Novo

CALLE TOSCANA

FONDACO
DEI TEDESCHI

SAN
APONAL

Campo
San Aponal

WC

**WALK
BEGINS**

**RIALTO
BRIDGE**

Campo
San
Silvestro

SAN
SILVESTRO

Rialto

Corte
Barzizza

SAN
BARTOLOMEO

To
San
Marco

PALAZZO
BARZIZZA

San
Silvestro

PALAZZO
DOLFIN-MANIN

PALAZZO
PAPADOPOLI

PALAZZO
BEMBO

SAN
SALVADOR

Canal

PALAZZO
DONÀ

TEATRO
GOLDONI

PALAZZO
MARTINENGO

PALAZZO
GRIMANI

PALAZZO
BENZON

PALAZZO
CURTI

Campo
San
Beneto

100 Meters

100 Yards

SAN MARCO

❶ Campo San Giacomo
❷ Produce Market
❸ Fish Market
❹ The Ruga
❺ Campo San Polo
❻ Church of San Polo
❼ Tragicomica Mask Shop

fish-shaped Venice. At #203, the Macelleria Equina shop sells horse (*cavallo*) and donkey (*asino*) meat. Continue along the canal, exploring all the produce stalls.

▶ *Follow your nose straight ahead (passing six alleyways on your left) until you see* Mercato del Pesce *on the brick wall of the open-air arcade that houses the...*

❸ Fish Market (Pescaria)

This market is especially vibrant and colorful in the morning. The open-air stalls have the catch of the day—Venice's culinary specialty. Find eels, scallops, crustaceans with five-inch antennae, and squid destined for tonight's risotto soaking in their own ink. This is the Venice that has existed for centuries: Workers toss boxes of fish from delivery boats while shoppers step from the *traghetto* into the action. It's a good peek at workaday Venice. Shoppers are exacting and expect to know if the fish is fresh or frozen, farmed or wild. Local fish are small and considered particularly tasty because of the high concentration of salt at this end of the Adriatic. Any salmon you see are farmed, mostly from northern Europe. It's not unusual to pay €30 per kilo (about 2.2 pounds) for the best fish.

In the courtyard between market buildings, locate a square white Istrian stone on the wall between two arches. It lists the minimum length permitted for a fish to be sold. Sardines must be seven centimeters; *peocio* (mussels) must be three centimeters. (Below that, someone has added a penis joke.)

Now walk away from the water to the end of the fish market. You're on Campo de la Becarie (Butchers Square). Several of my

Many Venetians shop daily in this market.

The Ruga cuts through the San Polo area.

favorite *cicchetti* bars line up along Calle de le Do Spade (which we'll pass in just a moment—see page 162).

When you're ready, follow Ruga dei Spezieri (Spicers Road) back toward Rialto. Along the way, pop into Antica Drogheria Mascari (on the right at #380), which hides a vast *enoteca* holding 600 different Italian wines arranged by region, plus spices and lots of gifty edibles.

▶ *At the end of Ruga dei Spezieri, you'll see a sign for* Ruga Vechia San Giovanni. *Turn right along it.*

❹ The Ruga

This busy street is lined with shops that get progressively less touristy and more practical. As you walk, you'll see fewer trinkets and more clothes, bread, shoes, watches, shampoo, and underwear.

▶ *The Ruga changes names as you go. Just keep heading basically straight (little jogs are OK). When in doubt, follow signs pointing to Ferrovia (train station). You'll cross one bridge, then shortly after come to...*

❺ Campo San Polo

One of the largest squares in Venice, Campo San Polo is shaped like an amphitheater, with its church tucked away in the corner (just ahead of you). Antica Birraria la Corte, a fine and family-friendly pizzeria/ristorante, is located at the far side (see page 165). The square's amphitheater shape was determined by a curved canal at the base of the buildings. Today, the former canal is now a *rio terà*—a street made of landfill. A few rare trees grace the square, as do rare benches occupied by grateful locals. In the summer, bleachers and a screen are erected for open-air movies.

▶ *On the square is the...*

❻ Church of San Polo (S. Paolo Apostolo)

This church, one of the oldest in Venice, dates from the ninth century (English description at ticket desk). The wooden, boat-shaped ceiling recalls the earliest basilicas built after Rome's fall. While the church is skippable for many, art enthusiasts visit to see Tintoretto's *Last Supper,* Giovanni Battista Tiepolo's *Virgin Appearing to St. John of Nepomuk* and his son Domenico's *Stations of the Cross,* and Veronese's *Betrothal of the Virgin with Angels.*

Tintoretto's *Last Supper*—one of the less-touristed versions of this scene found in Venice

▸ *From the Church of San Polo, continue about 200 yards (following Ferrovia signs). You'll cross a bridge, jog left when you have to, then right, onto Calle dei Nomboli. On the right at #2800, directly across the alley from the Casa Goldoni museum, you'll see the...*

❼ Tragicomica Mask Shop

One of Venice's best mask stores, Tragicomica is also a workshop that offers a glimpse into the process of mask-making. You'll see Walter, Alessandra, and Giuliana hard at work.

Venice's masks have always been a central feature of the celebration of Carnevale—the local pre-Lent, Mardi Gras-like blowout. (The translation of Carnevale is "goodbye to meat," referring to the lean days of Lent.) Many masks are patterned after standard characters of the theater style known as *commedia dell'arte*: the famous trickster Harlequin, the beautiful and cunning Columbina, the country bumpkin Pulcinella (who later evolved into the Punch of marionette shows), and the solemn, long-nosed Doctor (*dottore*). For more on masks, see page 196.

▸ *Continuing along, cross the bridge and veer right, passing San Tomà Church and its square. You'll soon see purple signs directing you to Scuola Grande di San Rocco (see page 139). Follow these until you bump into the back end of the Frari Church. Here, you can step inside the cool church, take a seat at a pew, and enjoy one of the city's most delightful art experiences. For more on the church, ✪ see the Frari Church Tour chapter on page 83.*

St. Mark's to San Zaccaria Walk

San Zaccaria, one of the oldest churches in Venice, is just a few minutes on foot from St. Mark's Square. The church features a Bellini altarpiece and a submerged crypt that might be the oldest place in Venice. This short walk gets you away from the bustle of St. Mark's, includes a stroll along the waterfront, and brings you right back to where you started.

ORIENTATION

Length of This Walk: Allow about an hour for a leisurely walk (though the actual distance is short), including a stop inside the church.

Church of San Zaccaria: Free, €1.50 to enter crypt, €0.50 coin to illuminate Bellini's altarpiece, open Mon-Sat 10:00-12:00 & 16:00-18:00, Sun 16:00-18:00 only. Mass is held daily at 18:30 and Sun also at 10:00 and 12:00.

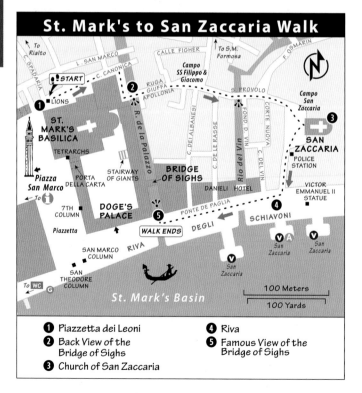

St. Mark's to San Zaccaria Walk

1. Piazzetta dei Leoni
2. Back View of the Bridge of Sighs
3. Church of San Zaccaria
4. Riva
5. Famous View of the Bridge of Sighs

THE WALK BEGINS

❶ St. Mark's—Piazzetta dei Leoni

Facing St. Mark's Basilica, start in the small square to the left of the church (Piazzetta dei Leoni), with the 18th-century stone lions that kids love to play on. See those drains in the pavement? You're standing on a cistern, fed by four drains.

Notice the nicely restored north side of the basilica, with fine 14th-century reliefs. Notice also the worship-only entrance below the exquisite Porta dei Fiori. To the left, high above the tomb of Daniele Manin, the great 19th-century Italian and Venetian patriot, is a statue with Baby Jesus on his shoulder. That's St. Christopher, patron saint of us travelers.

The white Neoclassical building at the far east end of the square (built in 1834, when Venice was under Austrian rule) houses the offices of Venice's "patriarch," the special title given to the local bishop. In the 1950s, this is where the future Pope John XXIII presided as Venice's patriarch and cardinal. The popular, warm-hearted cardinal went on to become the "Sixties Pope," who oversaw major reforms in the Catholic Church (Vatican II). You'll see a plaque dedicated to "Papa Giovanni XXIII," the man locals still refer to as "Il Papa Buono"—the good pope.

▶ *Head east along Calle de la Canonica, past a fine English-language bookstore, then turn right and circle behind the basilica. Passing some of the sexiest gondoliers in town, you'll reach a bridge with a...*

The lions of Piazzetta dei Leoni
Bridge of Sighs—and bridge of sightseers

❷ View of the Bridge of Sighs

This lesser-known view of the Bridge of Sighs also lets you see the tourists who are ogling it, with cameras cocked. You can just see the Lady Justice relief (centered above the windows), with her sword and scales—a reminder that the courts were to the right and the prison to the left.

On the basilica side of the bridge is a common sight in neighborhood Venice: a street-side altarpiece and donation box. As the street signs tell you, the bridge you're on marks the boundary between two traditional neighborhoods, the *sestiere* (district) of San Marco and that of Castello. Throughout this walk, you'll pass relics of a fast-fading era: newspaper stands, public telephones, and a 24-hour cigarette vending machine.

▸ *Continue east, passing through a lively, small square. You'll cross another bridge with a view of a "Modern Bridge of Sighs," which connects two wings of the exclusive Danieli Hotel. Continue east another 50 yards, through the Gothic gate of what was once a cloistered Benedictine convent, and into a square where you see the...*

❸ Church of San Zaccaria

Back in the ninth century, when Venice was just a collection of wooden houses and before there was a St. Mark's Basilica, a stone church and monastery stood here. This is where the doges worshipped, public spectacles occurred, and sacred relics were kept. Today's structure dates mostly from the 15th century.

The tall facade by Mauro Codussi (who also did the Clock Tower in St. Mark's Square) and others is early Renaissance. The "vertical" effect produced by the four support pillars that rise up to an arched crown is tempered by the horizontal, many-layered stories and curved shoulders.

In the northwest corner of Campo San Zaccaria (near where you entered) is a plaque from 1620 listing all the things that were prohibited "in this square" (*in questo campo*), including games, obscenities, dishonesty, and robbery, all "under grave penalty" (*sotto gravis pene*).

▸ *Enter the church. The second chapel on the right holds the...*

Body of Zechariah (S. Zaccaria)

Of the two bodies in the chapel, the lower one in the glass case is the

Bellini's *Madonna* (center) sits in a fake niche that appears to be an extension of the church.

reputed body of Zechariah, the father of John the Baptist. Back when mortal remains were venerated and thought to bring miracles to the faithful, Venice was proud to own the bones of St. Zechariah ("San Zaccaria," also known as Zacharias).

▶ *The church is blessed with fine art. On the opposite side of the nave (second chapel on the left), you'll find...*

Giovanni Bellini—Madonna and Child with Saints (1505)

Mary and the baby, under a pavilion, are surrounded by various saints interacting in a so-called *Sacra Conversazione* (holy conversation), which in this painting is more like a quiet meditation. The saints' mood is melancholy, with lidded eyes and downturned faces. A violinist angel plays a sad solo at Mary's feet.

This is one of the last of Bellini's paintings in the *sacra conversazione* formula, the newer type of altarpiece that liberated the Virgin, Child, and saints from the separate cells of the older triptych style. Compare this to his other variations on this theme in the Accademia (✪ see page 132) and Frari Church (✪ see the Frari Church Tour). The life-size saints stand in an imaginary extension of the church—the pavilion's painted columns match those of the real church. We see a glimpse of trees and a cloudy sky beyond. Bellini establishes a 3-D effect using floor tiles. The four saints pose symmetrically, and there's a harmony in the big blocks of richly colored robes—blue, green, red, white, and yellow. A cool white light envelops the whole scene, creating a holy ambience. (To add even more light, drop a €0.50 coin in the box in front of the altar.)

The ever-innovative Bellini was productive until the end of his long life—he painted this masterpiece at age 75. The German artist

Albrecht Dürer said of him: "He is very old, and still he is the best painter of them all."

▶ *On the right-hand side of the nave is the entrance (€1.50 entry fee) to the...*

Crypt

Before you descend into the crypt, the first room (Chapel of Sant'Atanasio) contains **Tintoretto's *Birth of John the Baptist*** (c. 1560s, on the altar), which tells the backstory of Zechariah. In the background, old Zechariah's wife, Elizabeth, props herself up in bed while nurses hold and coo over her newborn son, little John the Baptist. The birth was a miracle, as she was past childbearing age. On the far right, Zechariah—the star of this church—witnesses the heavens opening up, bringing this miracle to earth.

The five **gold thrones** (displayed in this room or one of the next rooms) were once seats for doges. Every Easter, the current doge would walk from St. Mark's Square to this religious center and thank the nuns of San Zaccaria for giving the land for the square.

The small next room contains religious objects as well as an engraving of the doge parading into Campo San Zaccaria.

Next comes the Chapel of San Tarasio, dominated by an impressive 15th-century prickly gold altarpiece by Antonio Vivarini. The predella (seven small scenes beneath the altarpiece) may be by Paolo Veneziano, the 14th-century grandfather of Venetian painting. Look down through glass in the floor to see the 12th-century mosaic floor from the original church. In fact, these rooms were parts of the earlier churches.

Finally, go downstairs to the **crypt**—the foundation of a church built in the 10th century. The crypt is low and the water table high, so the room is often flooded, submerging the bases of the columns. Venice has battled rising water levels since the fifth century. It's a weird experience, calling up echoes of the Dark Ages.

Flooding (the *acqua alta*) affects parts of Venice about 100 times a year, usually in winter. It occurs when an unusually high tide combines with strong sirocco winds from Africa that push the water toward Venice, causing a surging storm tide. In 2003, the city began construction on a system of underwater gates near the Lido, hoping to block the tidal surge. Still, some worry that—with global warming

San Zaccaria crypt is often flooded.

Grand hotels along the Riva promenade

and rising sea levels—Venice's battle against the sea is not over, and the water seems to be winning.

▶ *Emerge from the Church of San Zaccaria into the small campo. Before leaving the campo, check out the small art gallery on the left (free), the thirst-quenching water fountain, and the pink Carabinieri police station (a former convent), marked by the Italian flag. Then exit the square at the far end, and head south—past that cigarette machine— until you pop out at the waterfront, right on the...*

❹ Riva

The waterfront promenade known as the Riva was built not for tourists but as part of the port of San Marco. Until recently, big ships tied up here. Today it's lined with some of the town's finest hotels and provides a great view of the Church of San Giorgio Maggiore (one stop away on vaporetto #2).

The big equestrian monument depicts Victor Emmanuel II, who helped lead Italy to unification and became the country's first king in 1861. Beyond that (over the bridge) is the four-columned La Pietà Church, where Antonio Vivaldi once conducted music. Five bridges farther along (not visible from here) are the Arsenale and Naval Museum (described on page 145).

The Riva is lined with many of Venice's most famous luxury hotels. For a peek at the *most* famous and luxurious, turn right, cross over one bridge, and nip into the **Danieli Hotel.** Tuck in your shirt, stand tall and aristocratic, and (with all the confidence of a guest) be swept by the revolving door into the sumptuous interior of what was once the Gothic Palazzo Dandolo. As you check out the Danieli's restaurant menu (that's why you're there, isn't it?), admire the lobby, the old-style chandeliers, water-taxi drive-up entrance, and the occasional celebrity. Since 1820, the Neo-Gothic Danieli has been Venice's most exclusive hotel. Exquisite as all this is, it still gets flooded routinely in the winter.

▶ *Facing the water, turn right and head west toward St. Mark's Square. The commotion atop a little bridge marks the...*

❺ Famous View of the Bridge of Sighs

The Bridge of Sighs connects the Doge's Palace (left) with the doge's prison (right). The bridge let justice be very swift indeed, as convicted criminals could, upon sentencing, be escorted directly from the palace's secretive courtroom to prison, without being seen in public.

Notice the beefy bars on the prison. There were no windows, so throughout the year it would alternate between very hot and very cold. The top floor, below the lead roof, was nicknamed "The Oven." While designed for 300 people, the prison routinely held 500.

From this historic bridge (according to romantic legend), prisoners took one last look at Venice before entering the dark and unpleasant prisons. And sighed. Lord Byron picked up on the legend in the early 1800s and gave the bridge its famous nickname, making this sad little span a big stop on the Grand Tour. Look high up on your left—while that rogue Casanova wrote of the bridge in his memoirs, he was actually imprisoned here in the Doge's Palace.

Nowadays, while the bridge is a human traffic jam of gawking tourists during the day, it remains breathtakingly romantic in the lonely late-night hours.

▶ *Your tour's over. (By the way, if you need some quick cash, this is a great place to pick a pocket. There's lots of bumping, and everyone's distracted...)*

Sights

Venice's greatest sight is the city itself. As well as seeing world-class museums and buildings, make time to wander narrow lanes, linger over a meal, glide through the canals on a gondola, or enjoy evening magic on St. Mark's Square.

Remember that some of Venice's biggest sights (marked with a ✪) are described in much more detail in the individual walks and tours chapters. Also, one of Venice's most unique "sights"—a gondola ride—is covered on page 198.

Use my sightseeing tips to avoid crowds and lines at St. Mark's Square, the Basilica, and the Doge's Palace. A Museum Pass may save you a little money. For more sightseeing tips, ✪ see the Practicalities chapter.

And finally, remember that although Venice can be crowded and stressful, the city prides itself on its gentility and grace under pressure. Be flexible.

Venice

To Mestre &
Mainland

To Ghetto &
Guglie Bridge

SAN
GEREMIA

SAN
MARCUOLA

SCALZI

LISTA DI SPAGNA

Grand Canal

SANTA
LUCIA
STATION
(FERROVIA)

SAN ZAN
DEGOLÀ

BEMBO

To
Tronchetto
& Mainland

SCALZI
BRIDGE

SAN SIMEONE
GRANDE

SAN SIMEONE
PICCOLO

SAN
GIACOMO

PALAZZO
MOCENIGO

To Stazione Marittima
(Main Cruise Dock) &
Tronchetto (Parking)

CALATRAVA
BRIDGE

SANTA CROCE

SAN

GARAGE

Piazzale
Roma

CA'AMAI

Campo
San Stin

PEOPLE MOVER

BUS
STATION

SAN NICOLO
DA TOLENTINO

SAN
ROCCO

TINTORETTO

FRARI

Campo
San Polo

SAN
POLO

SCUOLA
SAN ROCCO

SAONERI

SAN
TOMA

SAN
PANTALON

CALLE LARGA
FOSCARI

SANTA
MARGARITA

T

A

CA'
FOSCARI

Campo
Santa
Margarita

CA'
REZZONICO

PALAZZO
GRASSI

SANTA MARIA
DEI CARMINI

Campo
San Barnaba

SAN
BARNABA

Campo
San
Stefano

OGNISSANTI

DORSODURO

TOLETTA

CORFU

ACCADEMIA
BRIDGE

SANTA MARTA
CRUISE DOCK

SAN
BASILIO
CRUISE DOCK

SAN
TROVASO

ACCADEMIA
GALLERY

WC

AGNESE

N

RIO TERA
FOSCARINI

200 Meters

200 Yards

FOND. ZATTERE AL PONTE LONGO

A

ZATTERE

Giudecca Canal

To San Michele, Murano, Burano & Torcello

Lagoon

SANTA MARIA MADALENA

SAN STAE

CA' PESARO

SAN FELICE

CA' D'ORO

SANTI APOSTOLI

Campo Santi Apostoli

SAN CANZIAN

HOSPITAL

SAN CASSIAN

FISH MARKET

Campo de le Becarie

PRODUCE MARKET

COLLEONI STATUE

SANTI GIOVANNI E PAOLO (SAN ZANIPOLO)

POLO

RIALTO BRIDGE

Campo San Aponal

SAN SILVESTRO

Campo San Bartolomeo

SAN LIO

Campo Santa Maria Formosa

SAN LORENZO

SAL SAN LIO

SANTA MARIA FAVA

TEATRO GOLDONI

SAN SALVADOR

MERCERIE

SCUOLA DALMATIA

CASTELLO

Campo San Luca

SAN ZULIAN

Campo Manin

MERCERIE

SAN ZACCARIA

SCALA CONTARINI DEL BOVOLO

FABERI

ST. MARK'S

BRIDGE OF SIGHS

LA PIETA

Campo S. Anzolo

CORRER MUSEUM

CAMPANILE

RIVA DEGLI SCHIAVONI

LA FENICE OPERA HOUSE

Piazza San Marco

SAN MARCO

DOGE'S PALACE

To Public Gardens & Sant'Elena

Campo San Maurizio

22 MARZO

SAN MOISE

SAN MARCO & SAN THEODORE COLUMNS

Campo Santa Maria Zobenigo

Grand Canal

St. Mark's Basin

To Lido

LA SALUTE

PUNTA DELLA DOGANA MUSEUM (CUSTOMS HOUSE)

SAN GIORGIO MAGGIORE

PEGGY GUGGENHEIM COLLECTION

SPIRITO SANTO

SAN GIORGIO

Near St. Mark's Square

Venice's historic heart stretches north from St. Mark's Square to the Rialto Bridge, east to the Church of San Zaccaria, and west to La Fenice Opera House. The handiest vaporetto stops are San Marco-Vallaresso (100 yards west of the square) and the four docks of San Zaccaria (150 yards east of the square).

This area can be very crowded at midday (10:00-17:00), so try to do your sightseeing here early or late. It's another world altogether at night—lantern-lit magic under a ceiling of stars.

Use two of my walks to lace together sights in this area:

✪ St. Mark's to Rialto Loop Walk
✪ St. Mark's to San Zaccaria Walk

▲▲▲ St. Mark's Square (Piazza San Marco)

This grand square is surrounded by splashy, historic buildings and music-filled cafés. By day it's a world of pigeons and tourists. At night, it's your private rendezvous with the romantic Venetian past.

✪ See the St. Mark's Square Tour chapter.

▲▲▲ St. Mark's Basilica (Basilica di San Marco)

This one-of-a-kind church is adorned with Byzantine-style domes outside and gold mosaics inside. St. Mark's bones lie under the altar. Three separate museums in the church show off rare treasures, a Golden Altarpiece, and the four bronze horse statues.

✪ See the St. Mark's Basilica Tour chapter.

▲▲▲ Doge's Palace (Palazzo Ducale)

The seat of the Venetian government and home of its ruling duke, or doge, this was the most powerful half-acre in Europe for 400 years. Walk through once-lavish (now sparse) rooms wallpapered by great Venetian painters, learn about Venetian government, and finish by crossing the Bridge of Sighs into the notorious prison.

✪ See the Doge's Palace Tour chapter.

▲ Bridge of Sighs

This much-photographed bridge connects the Doge's Palace with the prison. Supposedly, a condemned man would cross this bridge, take one last look at the glory of Venice, and sigh. Though overhyped, the Bridge of Sighs is undeniably tingle-worthy, especially after dark.

Sightseeing in the St. Mark's Square area is especially crowded at midday.

For more on the bridge, see the St. Mark's to San Zaccaria Walk chapter and the Doge's Palace Tour chapter.

▲▲ Correr Museum (Museo Correr)

A doge's hat, gleaming statues by Canova, and paintings by the illustrious Bellini family—for some people, that's a major museum; for others, an historical bore. This uncrowded museum gives a good overview of Venetian history and art, is a quiet refuge with views over tourist-crowded St. Mark's Square, and is included anyway in your Doge's Palace ticket.

The first few rooms highlight Venice's greatest homegrown sculptor, Antonio Canova (1757-1822). He created high-polished, slender, beautiful figures—often arranged in groups that are interesting from many angles—and combined the cool lines of classicism with the romantic sentiment of Venice. In *Orpheus and Eurydice* (1775-1776), the Greek poet is leading his beloved back from hell when she's suddenly tugged backward. Orpheus smacks his forehead in horror, but he must continue on, leaving an empty space between them.

In Rooms 6-14, the world of the doges comes to life with doge portraits and a single-horned doge cap. Room 11 has a Venetian ducat—99 percent pure gold, worth about $1,000—that was once Europe's

Correr Museum—First Floor

To St. Mark's Basilica

To Piazzetta & Doge's Palace Entrance

CAMPANILE

To Marciana Nat'l Library

NATIONAL ARCHAEO-LOGICAL MUSEUM

Not to scale

Piazza

TOURISTS →

18 | 19

17

16

15

STAIRS TO SECOND FLOOR

14

San

13 WC

THE SEA → 12

COINS → 11

10

Marco

LIBRARY → 9

8

DOGES → 7

6

PIGEONS

CANOVA

5

IX VIII

4

VII

ENTRY THROUGH PASSAGEWAY FROM PIAZZA SAN MARCO & UP STAIRS

3

VI

SISSI ROOMS

V

CAFÉ

LOGGIA 3

NAPOLEONICA 3

IV

ROOM 1

BALLROOM 2

I II III

STAIRS TICKETS

CANOVA

To WC

To San Marco Vaporetto Stops & Accademia

strongest currency. Room 12 displays models of the sleek, oar- and wind-powered warships that ruled the waves. The Arsenale (Room 13) could crank out a galley a day. Room 14's old maps illustrate how little the city has changed—find your hotel on Barbari's big map from 1500.

Rooms 15-18 display armor and weapons. You can detour into the National Archaeological Museum (so-so classical statues) and the impressive Marciana National Library (globes, manuscripts, and ceiling paintings), both included with admission.

The second floor traces Venetian painting from golden Byzantine icons to Florentine-inspired 3-D to Venice's trademark soft-focus beauty. Room 36 highlights the family that single-handedly brought Venetian painting into the Renaissance—the Bellinis. The famous Giovanni Bellini (c. 1430-1516) specialized in forever-young, pastel-colored Virgins holding rosy-cheeked Baby Jesuses. Finally, in Room 38, Carpaccio's well-known *Two Venetian Gentlewomen* (c. 1490) are surrounded by exotic pets and amusements, absentmindedly awaiting their menfolk. Fascinating stuff, but my eyes—like theirs—are starting to glaze...

▸ *€20 combo-ticket also includes the Doge's Palace, also covered by Museum Pass. Open daily 10:00-19:00, Nov-March until 17:00, last entry one hour before closing. Bag check free and mandatory for bags bigger than a large purse, elegant café, enter at far end of square directly opposite basilica. Tel. 041-240-5211, http://correr.visitmuve.it.*

▲ Campanile (Campanile di San Marco)

This dramatic bell tower replaced a shorter tower, part of the original fortress that guarded the entry to the Grand Canal. That tower crumbled into a pile of bricks in 1902, a thousand years after it was built. Ride the elevator 325 feet up for the best view in Venice (especially at sunset). For an ear-shattering experience, be on top when the bells ring. The golden archangel Gabriel at the top always faces the wind. Beat the crowds and enjoy the crisp morning air at 9:00 or the cool evening breeze at 18:00.

▸ *€8. Open daily 8:30-21:00, Sept-mid-Oct until sunset, mid-Oct-April 9:30-17:30, last entry 45 minutes before closing, may close during thunderstorms, audioguide-€3. Tel. 041-522-4064, www.basilicasanmarco.it.*

For more on the Campanile, ✪ see the St. Mark's Square Tour chapter.

Two of Venice's best views are from the towers of St. Mark's (left) and San Giorgio (right).

La Fenice Opera House (Gran Teatro alla Fenice)

For 200 years, great operas and famous divas debuted here, in one of Europe's most famous opera houses. Then in 1996, an arson fire completely gutted the theater. But La Fenice ("The Phoenix") has risen from the ashes. To see the results at their most glorious, attend an evening performance. The theater box office is open daily 10:00-17:00 (tel. 041-2424, www.teatrolafenice.it).

You can also tour the opera house during the day. All you really see is the theater itself; there's no "backstage" tour of dressing rooms, or an opera museum. However, the auditorium, ringed with box seats, is impressive: pastel blue with sparkling gold filigree, muses depicted on the ceiling, and a starburst chandelier.

For more on the opera house, ✪ see the St. Mark's to Rialto Loop Walk chapter.

▶ *€10 tour includes dry audioguide. Generally open daily 9:30-18:00, but can vary wildly, depending on the performance schedule—to confirm, call box office number above or check www.festfenice.com. La Fenice is on Campo San Fantin, 100 yards west of St. Mark's Square.*

▲ San Giorgio Maggiore

This is the dreamy church-topped island you can see from the waterfront by St. Mark's Square. It's worth a boat ride there for Palladio's architecture, Tintoretto's *Last Supper,* bell-tower views, and a pleasant escape from tourist-mobbed St. Mark's Square.

The facade—with its four tall columns topped by a triangular pediment—looks like a Greek temple. The architect Andrea Palladio (1508-1580), with his classical style, was hugely influential on

Best Views

- The soaring Campanile on St. Mark's Square
- The balcony of St. Mark's Basilica in the San Marco Museum
- Rialto Bridge, with a free, expansive view of the Grand Canal, along with a cooling breeze
- The luxury "mall" Fondaco dei Tedeschi, just north of the Rialto Bridge, with great Grand Canal views
- Accademia Bridge, overlooking the Grand Canal and dome of La Salute Church
- The Church of San Giorgio Maggiore's bell tower, with views back at downtown Venice and all around the lagoon
- The swanky bar of the Hilton Molino Stucky Hotel on Giudecca Island (free shuttle boat leaves from near the San Zaccaria-B vaporetto dock)

generations of architects in England and America. The bell tower echoes the Campanile in St. Mark's Square.

The interior is white and well-lit by clear glass, with a clarity and mathematical perfection that exudes the classical world.

On the wall to the right of the altar is a *Last Supper* (1592-1594) by Tintoretto. The table stretches diagonally away on a tiled floor, drawing us in. The scene is crowded—servants and cats mingle with wispy angels—and a blazing lamp radiates supernatural light. Your eyes go straight to a well-lit Christ, serving his faithful with both hands. In Tintoretto's *Manna from Heaven,* on the opposite wall, hungry Israelites gather God's heaven-sent bread.

Take the elevator up the bell tower for a stunning view. Looking north is Venice's famous skyline. Facing east across the lagoon, find the long, narrow island of Lido. Facing west is the nearby island of Giudecca. The old flour mill at the far end is now a Hilton hotel.

Finally, looking up, you see the bells that chime the hours. You've been warned.

▶ *Free entry to church, €6 for bell tower. Open daily 9:00-19:00, Nov-March 8:30-18:00. The bell-tower elevator runs until 20 minutes before closing, not accessible during Sun services. Bell tower can get crowded at midday. An untouristed harborside café is 150 yards around the left of the church. Get to San Giorgio Maggiore via a five-minute ride on vaporetto #2 from San Zaccaria (6/hour, €5 special vaporetto ticket, usually from dock B, direction: Tronchetto).*

Accademia and Dorsoduro

The Accademia Bridge, one of the city's key landmarks, is the gateway to the Dorsoduro neighborhood. The Dorsoduro is somewhat less touristed, more intimate, and filled with some of Venice's best art venues. The bridge is a 10-minute walk from St. Mark's Square (vaporetto: Accademia or Zattere).

▲▲Accademia (Galleria dell'Accademia)

Venice's top art museum is a chronological overview of artists whose colorful works are found all over town.

Start with medieval altarpieces in Room 1, whose gold-leaf backgrounds and "icon"-ic faces show Venice's Byzantine roots. In Room 2, Giovanni Bellini's *Enthroned Madonna with Child* (c. 1480) brings Mary down from her golden heaven into the same spacious, 3-D world we inhabit. Bellini created Madonnas with creamy complexions and soft outlines, bathed in his trademark golden haze. In Giorgione's *The Tempest* (c. 1505, Room 4), the serene landscape is about to be shattered by an approaching storm, the center of the composition.

Room 10 features Venetian art at its peak. Veronese's enormous *Feast in the House of Levi* (1573) fills your field of vision with a Venetian party. Everyone's dressed to kill, servants bring on the food, and dogs roam free. The bawdy work was originally called the *Last Supper,* until

Veronese's colorful *Feast in the House of Levi* captures Venice's Renaissance-era joie de vivre.

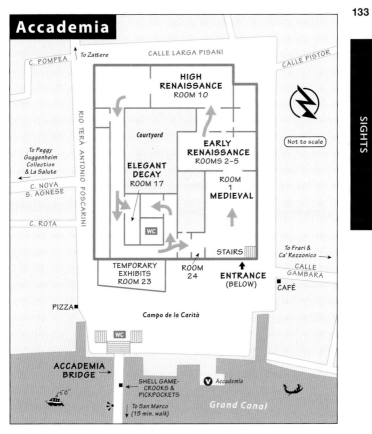

Accademia

CALLE LARGA PISANI

To Zattere

C. POMPEA

CALLE PISTOR

HIGH RENAISSANCE
ROOM 10

RIO TERA ANTONIO FOSCARINI

Courtyard

To Peggy Guggenheim Collection & La Salute

C. NOVA S. AGNESE

EARLY RENAISSANCE
ROOMS 2-5

ELEGANT DECAY
ROOM 17

ROOM 1
MEDIEVAL

(Not to scale)

SIGHTS

C. ROTA

WC

STAIRS

To Frari & Ca' Rezzonico →

CALLE GAMBARA

TEMPORARY EXHIBITS
ROOM 23

ROOM 24

ENTRANCE
(BELOW)

CAFÉ

PIZZA ■

Campo de la Carità

WC

ACCADEMIA BRIDGE →

SHELL GAME- CROOKS & PICKPOCKETS

ⓥ *Accademia*

To San Marco
(15 min. walk)

Grand Canal

Veronese was hauled before the Inquisition. Rather than change the painting, he just changed the title.

Titian painted his *Pietà* (c. 1573) to hang over his own tomb. The canvas is dark and somber, a mess of rough, proto-"Impressionist" brushstrokes. A dramatic line of motion sweeps up diagonally, culminating in Mary Magdalene, who flings her arm and howls. The kneeling old man is Titian himself. In Tintoretto's *The Removal of St. Mark's Body* (1562-1566), Venetian merchants whisk away the body of

St. Mark, seemingly bringing it out of the picture frame and into our world.

Rooms 11 and beyond chronicle Venice's elegant years of decline. G. B. Tiepolo (*Discovery of the True Cross,* c. 1745) took Venice's colorful, theatrical style and plastered it on the ceilings of Europe's Baroque palaces. As Venice became Europe's number-one tourist attraction, Venetian artists painted "postcard" scenes for wealthy visitors. Canaletto gave Venice a sharp-focus, wide-lens, camera's-eye perspective, while Guardi sweetened up the city with an Impressionistic haze of messy brushwork.

On your way out (Room 24), don't miss Titian's colorful *Presentation of the Virgin* (1534-1538). Titian painted the work especially for this room; notice how the door on the left, added later, cuts into the masterpiece. The painting sums up the style of the Venetian Renaissance: bright colors, big canvases, 3-D realism, Renaissance architecture, and colorful scenes of everyday life in Venice. Now go out into Venice and enjoy the real thing.

▶ *€12. Open Mon 8:15-14:00, Tue-Sun until 19:15, last entry one hour before closing. Visit early or late to miss the crowds. Dull audioguide-€6. Major renovation is nearing its end, so be flexible. Located next to Accademia Bridge. Tel. 041-522-2247, www.gallerieaccademia.org.*

▲▲ Peggy Guggenheim Collection

One of Europe's best early-20th-century modern art museums is housed in the American heiress' former retirement palazzo. Visitors get a glimpse into Peggy's fascinating life, her home, and art by artists she knew personally as friend, lover, and patron.

In 1920, young Peggy Guggenheim (1898-1979) traveled to Paris, where she lived a bohemian life with avant-garde artists. In the 1930s, her friend Marcel Duchamp and boyfriend Samuel (*Waiting for Godot*) Beckett encouraged her to collect modern art. She spent the war years in America, where her New York art gallery inspired a generation. When her memoirs were published, Peggy became a celebrity. She was unconventional and larger than life, with a succession of lovers that made her a female Casanova.

In 1948, Peggy came "home" to Venice, renovating this small palazzo on the Grand Canal. It became a mecca for "Moderns," from composer Igor Stravinsky to actor Marlon Brando to writer Truman Capote to Beatle John Lennon and (Peggy's travel buddy) Yoko Ono.

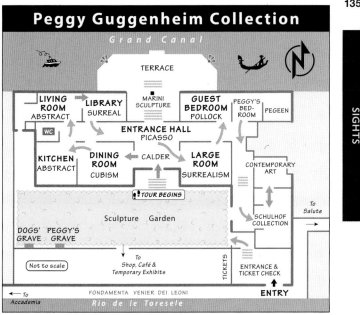

Peggy Guggenheim Collection

Grand Canal

TERRACE

MARINI SCULPTURE

LIVING ROOM
ABSTRACT

LIBRARY
SURREAL

GUEST BEDROOM
POLLOCK

PEGGY'S BED-ROOM

PEGEEN

WC

ENTRANCE HALL
PICASSO

KITCHEN
ABSTRACT

DINING ROOM
CUBISM

CALDER

LARGE ROOM
SURREALISM

CONTEMPORARY ART

TOUR BEGINS

Sculpture Garden

SCHULHOF COLLECTION

To Salute

DOGS' GRAVE

PEGGY'S GRAVE

Not to scale

To Shop, Café & Temporary Exhibits

TICKETS

ENTRANCE & TICKET CHECK

To Accademia

FONDAMENTA VENIER DEI LEONI

ENTRY

Rio de le Toresele

Today, though most of the furniture is gone, it's easy to get a feel for the place as Peggy's home. The rooms have much the same art as hung here in Peggy's day (as old photos attest). In the entrance hall, you can picture Peggy greeting her guests—standing under the Calder mobile, flanked by Picasso paintings, holding her yapping dogs, and wearing her Mondrian-print dress and "Catwoman" sunglasses. In the dining room, the wood table is original. The bedroom displays the silver headboard by Calder that originally adorned Peggy's bed. Nearby are childlike paintings done by Peggy's daughter, Pegeen.

The collection's strength is in Abstract, Surrealist, and Abstract Expressionist works. Highlights include Picasso's art-shattering Cubist masterpiece, *The Poet*. Picasso's *On the Beach* was Peggy's favorite painting. Marcel Duchamp's *Nude* is a blurred self-portrait of Peggy's mentor. Abstract works by Kandinsky and Mondrian were highly influential on America's young Abstract Expressionists. You'll see Surrealist works by Yves Tanguy (Peggy's boyfriend) and Max Ernst (her husband). In Ernst's *The Antipope,* the horse-headed nude in red is supposedly a portrait of Peggy. Other Surrealist highlights include an ominous suburban scene by Magritte and a photorealistic dreamscape by Dalí. Jackson Pollock—aka "Jack the Dripper"—became famous largely thanks to Peggy's support. Outside in the sculpture garden, find the graves of Peggy's Lhasa Apso dogs—"Here Lie My Beloved Babies"—with Peggy's ashes buried humbly alongside.

End your visit on the terrace, where Peggy would sip her morning coffee with this incredible view. The exuberant equestrian statue by Marini faces the Grand Canal, spreads his arms wide, and tosses his head back in sheer joy, with an eternal hard-on for the city of Venice.

▶ *€15, usually includes temporary exhibits. Open Wed-Mon 10:00-18:00, closed Tue. Audioguide-€7. Pricey café, art galleries nearby. Easy to reach by vaporetto (Accademia or Salute). Tel. 041-240-5411, www. guggenheim-venice.it.*

▲ La Salute Church (Santa Maria della Salute)

Where the Grand Canal opens up into the lagoon stands one of Venice's most distinctive landmarks. The white stone church has a steep, crown-shaped dome that rises above an octagonal structure. It's encrusted with Baroque scrolls and 125 statues, topped by the Virgin Mary. The church was dedicated to her—Santa Maria della Salute (Our Lady of Health)—by grateful survivors of the 1630 plague.

The architect, Baldassare Longhena (1598-1682), remade Venice in the Baroque style, and La Salute was his crowning achievement. He sank countless pilings (locals claim over a million) into the sandy soil to help support the mammoth dome.

Exuberant modern art at the Guggenheim

La Salute—impressive church, fine art

Inside, the church has a bright, healthy glow, well-lit from clear glass windows. The nave is circular, surrounded by chapels. At the main altar, marble statues tell the church's story: The Virgin (center) is approached for help by a kneeling, humble Lady Venice (left). Mary shows compassion and sends an angel baby (right) to drive away Old Lady Plague.

Artwork in the church includes three paintings by Luca Giordano (in the three side chapels to the right of the altar), Titian's *Pentecost* (the chapel to the left of the altar), and works by Tintoretto and Titian in the (not always open) Sacristy.

▶ *Free entry to church, €4 for Sacristy. Open daily 9:00-12:00 & 15:00-17:30. It's a 10-minute walk from the Accademia Bridge, or reach by vaporetto (Salute stop). Service with organ music Mon-Thu at 15:30; Sun organ performance at 11:45. Tel. 041-274-3298, www.seminariovenezia.it.*

▲ Ca' Rezzonico (Museum of 18th-Century Venice)

Venice in the 1700s was the playground for Europe's aristocrats. Today, the Ca' Rezzonico (ret-ZON-ee-koh)—a palazzo on the Grand Canal—is the best place to experience the luxury-loving spirit of that decadent century. Wander under ceilings by Tiepolo and among Rococo furnishings, enjoying views of the canal and paintings by Guardi, Canaletto, and Longhi.

Start on the first floor, in the 5,600-square-foot Room 1, and imagine a glittering party of masked and powder-wigged dandies, beneath a trompe l'oeil ceiling. Room 2 has the first of several ceiling frescoes by Venice's own G. B. Tiepolo (1696-1770), the renowned decorator of Europe's palaces. Four white horses pull a chariot carrying Rezzonico family newlyweds. Tiepolo's zero-gravity scenes, bright colors, classical motifs, and sheer unbridled imagination made his frescoes blend seamlessly with ornate Rococo furniture. Room 4 has luminous pastel portraits and miniatures by the celebrated Venetian, Rosalba Carriera (1675-1757). Room 5 is decorated with Rococo tapestries, a mirror, and a cabinet door showing an opium smoker on his own little island paradise. Room 6, the Throne Room, has views over the Grand Canal and a Tiepolo ceiling that blows a hole in the roof, allowing angels to descend to honor old man Rezzonico. As the gang returns to heaven, the lady in blue leaves her leg dangling over the "edge" of the fake oval.

Rooms 7-12 have more period furniture, the carved-wood

fantasies of Andrea Brustolon (Room 11), and a sedan chair (Room 12) to transport the rich in red-velvet luxury.

The second floor features paintings. Room 13 has two "postcard" scenes of Venice by Canaletto. With a wide-angle lens and photographic clarity, he captures the canals, palaces, and hanging laundry of the city he loved. In Room 14, find scenes (by Tiepolo's son) of the hook-nosed bumpkin Pulcinella partying at Carnevale. Room 17 has a canvas by Guardi where men (wearing the traditional mask, three-cornered hat, and cowl) hit on masked prostitutes. As the 1700s was coming to an end, the decadent gaiety of Venice was giving way to modern democracy and the Industrial Age. Room 18 presents a startling contrast: Tiepolo's lush Rococo fantasy overhead and the straightforward scenes of everyday life by Pietro Longhi (1702-1785).

▶ *€10. Open Wed-Mon 10:00-18:00, Nov-March until 17:00, closed Tue; last entry one hour before closing. Audioguide-€4 or €6/2 people. Café, bag check required and free. Located at Ca' Rezzonico vaporetto stop, a 10-minute walk northwest of Accademia Bridge. Tel. 041-241-0100, http://carezzonico.visitmuve.it.*

▲ Punta della Dogana

This museum of contemporary art, housed in the former Customs House at the end of the Grand Canal, features cutting-edge 21st-century art in spacious rooms. This isn't Picasso and Matisse, or even Pollock and Warhol—those guys are ancient history. But if you're into the likes of Jeff Koons, Cy Twombly, Rachel Whiteread, and a host of newer artists, the museum is world-class. The displays change completely about every year, drawn from the museum's large collection—so large it also fills Palazzo Grassi, farther up the Grand Canal (vaporetto: San Samuele).

▶ *€20 (varies depending on exhibit). Open Wed-Mon 10:00-19:00, closed Tue, last entry one hour before closing. Audioguide sometimes available. Small café. Reach the Punta by vaporetto (Salute stop). Tel. 199-112-112 within Italy, 041-200-1057 from abroad, www.palazzograssi.it.*

Rialto

Rialto is the center of the Venice map and a major stop for vaporetto lines 1 and 2. The bridge is surrounded by tourist services and restaurants with great views and mediocre food. The east side of the bridge—along the busy Mercerie street to St. Mark's Square—is very touristy. The west leads into the less-touristed San Polo neighborhood, with the Frari Church and Scuola San Rocco. North of Rialto, along the Grand Canal, lie a few lesser sights (Ca' Pesaro, Palazzo Mocenigo), easily reached by vaporetto.

▲▲▲ Rialto Bridge

One of the world's most famous bridges, this distinctive and dramatic stone structure crosses the Grand Canal with a single confident span. The arcades along the top of the bridge help reinforce the structure... and offer some enjoyable shopping diversions, as does the market surrounding the bridge (produce, fish, and tourist goods).

✪ See the St. Mark's to Rialto Loop Walk chapter and the Rialto to Frari Church Walk chapter.

▲▲ Frari Church (Basilica di Santa Maria Gloriosa dei Frari)

My favorite art experience in Venice is seeing art in the setting for which it was designed—as it is at the Frari Church. You'll see the work of three great Renaissance masters—Donatello, Giovanni Bellini, and Titian—each showing worshippers the glory of God in human terms.

✪ See the Frari Church Tour chapter.

▲▲ Scuola San Rocco

Sometimes called "Tintoretto's Sistine Chapel," this lavish meeting hall has some 50 large, colorful paintings plastered to its walls and ceilings.

Start upstairs in the Albergo Hall (in the left corner of the Great Upper Hall), with scenes of Christ's Passion. In *Christ Before Pilate,* Jesus stands literally head and shoulders above his accusers, radiating innocence. The old man in white is Jacopo Tintoretto himself (1518-1594). The drama culminates in the expansive *Crucifixion.* Workers struggle to hoist crosses, mourners swoon, and riffraff gamble for Christ's clothes. Tintoretto focuses all the painting's lines of sight—the ladder on the ground, the angles of the crosses, the sloping hillsides—directly to the center, where Christ rises above it all, crucified but ultimately triumphant.

The huge Great Upper Hall has 34 enormous oil canvases in gold frames. They tell biblical history—Old Testament on the ceiling, New Testament along the walls—from Adam and Eve (at the Albergo end)

Scuola San Rocco is wallpapered with Tintoretto's *Crucifixion* and other Bible-themed works.

to the Ascension of Christ (at the altar end). Tintoretto painted a staggering 8,500 square feet—like covering a house, inside and out, with a tiny artist's brush. The paintings have Tintoretto's signature sense of drama, elongated bodies, light-dark contrast, diagonal compositions, bright metallic colors, and rough brushwork—creating scenes where the miraculous and the everyday mingle side by side.

The largest ceiling painting is *The Miracle of the Bronze Serpent.* The half-naked Israelites wrestle with snakes and writhe in pain. At the top of the pile, a young woman gestures toward Moses, who points to a bronze serpent that can heal all who gaze upon it. Walk around beneath the painting and it comes alive like a movie. Tintoretto was the Spielberg of his day, making the supernatural seem tangible. Nearby, in *Moses Strikes Water from the Rocks,* the thirsty Israelites scurry to catch the water, while Moses is the calm center of a wheel of activity.

In *The Last Supper* (on the wall to the left of the altar), a dog, a beggar, and a serving girl dominate the foreground, while the apostles dine in darkness. By emphasizing the ordinary elements, Tintoretto confirmed the faith of the San Rocco brotherhood—that God intervenes miraculously into our everyday lives.

▶ *€10. Open daily 9:30-17:30, audioguide-€5. Mirrors let you view the neck-breaking splendor. Located next to Frari Church. Get key for WCs from ticket clerk. Tel. 041-523-4864, www.scuolagrandesanrocco.it.*

Scuola San Rocco

Not to scale

GREAT UPPER HALL (UPSTAIRS)

CEILING

PAINTINGS

ALBERGO

STAIRS FROM/TO GROUND FLOOR

1 Christ Before Pilate
2 The Crucifixion
3 The Miracle of the Bronze Serpent
4 Moses Strikes Water from the Rocks
5 The Last Supper

▲ **Ca' Pesaro International Gallery of Modern Art**

This museum features 19th- and early-20th-century art in a 17th-century canalside palazzo. The highlights are in one large room: Klimt's beautiful/creepy *Judith II*, with eagle-talon fingers; Kandinsky's *White Zig Zags* (plus other recognizable shapes); the colorful *Nude in the Mirror* by Bonnard that flattens the 3-D scene into a 2-D pattern of rectangles; and Chagall's surprisingly realistic portrait of his hometown rabbi, *Rabbi #2* (a.k.a. *The Rabbi of Vitebsk*). The adjoining Room VII features small-scale works by Matisse, Max Ernst, Mark Tobey, and a Calder mobile.

▶ *€14. Open Tue-Sun 10:00-18:00, off-season until 17:00, closed Mon, last entry one hour before closing. Two-minute walk from San Stae vaporetto stop. Tel. 041-721-127, http://capesaro.visitmuve.it.*

Palazzo Mocenigo Costume Museum

Six rooms of a fine 17th-century mansion are filled with period furnishings, family portraits, ceilings painted (c. 1790) with family triumphs (the Mocenigos produced seven doges), Murano glass chandeliers in situ, and a paltry collection of costumes with sparse descriptions.

▶ €8. Open Tue-Sun 10:00-17:00, off-season until 16:00, closed Mon. Located a block inland from San Stae vaporetto stop. Tel. 041-721-798, http://mocenigo.visitmuve.it.

Near the Train Station (Ferrovia)

Jewish Ghetto

Venice's Jewish population once lived here, segregated from their non-Jewish neighbors. Today, the small neighborhood has centuries of history and a few Jewish-themed sights and eateries.

In medieval times, Jews were grudgingly allowed to do business in Venice, but in 1516, the doge restricted them to this area near the former foundry (*geto*). In time, the word "ghetto" caught on across Europe as a term for any segregated neighborhood.

Campo de Gheto Novo is the ghetto's center. To get there from the train station, walk five minutes to the Ponte de Guglie bridge over the Cannaregio Canal. Head 50 yards north to find a small covered alleyway (Calle del Gheto Vechio) near the Gam-Gam Kosher Restaurant. This street leads to Campo de Gheto Novo.

In the 1600s—the Golden Age of Venice's Jews—the Campo had 70 shops, and 5,000 Jews lived nearby, many packed into the six-story "skyscrapers" that still surround the square. To save space, the

Bridge to the once-segregated Jewish Ghetto

Calatrava's bridge to the 21st century

GHETTO

Rio de San Girolamo

FONDAMENTE DEI ORMESINI

PONTE DE GHETO NOVO

JEWISH SENIOR/ COMMUNITY CENTER

HOLOCAUST MEMORIALS

Rio del Batelo

PONTE DEL GHETO VECHIO

Campo de Gheto Novo

SOTOPORTEGO DEL GHETO NOVO

GHETO VECHIO

Rio di Gheto Novo

JEWISH MUSEUM & SYNAGOGUE

CALLE DEL FORNO

Corte Scala Mata

JEWISH COMMUNITY INFOPOINT

CALLE GHETO NOVISSIMO

Campo de la Scuola

FOND. DE GHETO NOVISSIMO

C. DEL TIRACANA

C. DE LA MASENA

To Rio Terà Farsetti & Rialto

GHETO VECHIO

To Ponte de le Guglie & Train Station

50 Meters

50 Yards

C. DEL CONTERIE

synagogues were built atop these tenements. The ghetto's two bridges were closed at night. In 1797, Napoleon ended the ghetto's isolation, and in the 1860s, the Italian republic granted Jews full citizenship.

Today the square is quiet. Only a few dozen Jews live in the former ghetto, and the Jewish people you may see are likely tourists. The main sight is the Jewish Museum (Museo Ebraico) at #2902b. It has silver menorahs, cloth covers for Torah scrolls, an overview of ghetto history, and guided tours of three old synagogues. From the Campo, you can see two synagogue exteriors (with their five windows) and three cistern wells. The large Casa Israelitica di Riposo is a Jewish senior/community center flanked by two different Holocaust memorials, marking where the Nazis rounded up 200 Jews for deportation. Only eight returned.

Backtrack across the bridge you came in on to find the information point at Calle del Gheto Vechio #1222, where Anat Shriki answers questions about ghetto history.

Return to the square and exit through Sotoportego del Gheto Novo. From here, it's easy to gaze on the tall tenement buildings and the easy-to-lock-up bridge, and picture life in the "fortress ghetto."

▸ *Jewish Museum–€8, open Sun-Fri 10:00-19:00, Oct-May closes at 17:30, closed Jewish holidays and Sat year-round. The €12 tours run hourly. Tel. 041-715-359, www.museoebraico.it.*

Calatrava Bridge (a.k.a. Ponte della Costituzione)

This modern bridge (2008) over the Grand Canal, designed by Spanish architect Santiago Calatrava, is just upstream from the train station. Only the fourth bridge over the Canal, it carries foot traffic between the train station and bus terminal at Piazzale Roma.

The bridge draws snorts from Venetians. Its construction was expensive (€11 million total), and the modern design runs counter to Venice's trademark medieval and Renaissance architecture. Adding practical insult to aesthetic injury, critics say the heavy bridge is crushing the centuries-old foundations at either end, threatening nearby buildings.

In the Fish's Tail (East of St. Mark's Square)

Get away from the crowds. Walk along the Riva (the waterfront promenade) or wind your way through back streets behind St. Mark's Basilica. Or take vaporetto line 1 east from San Zaccaria to Arsenale or Giardini. The sights I list are fine enough, but the real "sight" here is Venice's untouristed backyard.

▲ Scuola Dalmata di San Giorgio

This little-visited wood-paneled chapel is decorated with the world's best collection of paintings by Vittorio Carpaccio (1465-1526). They tell the story of St. George, who slew a dragon and metaphorically conquered paganism.

Carpaccio cuts right to the climax. In the first panel, George meets the dragon on the barren plain, charges forward, and jams his spear through the dragon's skull, to the relief of the damsel in distress (in red). George gets there a bit too late—notice half a damsel on the ground. Carpaccio places George and the dragon directly facing each other. Meanwhile, the center of the composition—where George meets dragon—is also the "vanishing point" that draws your eye to the distant horizon. Very clever.

In the next panel, George leads the bedraggled dragon (spear still in his head) before the thankful, wealthy pagan king and queen. Next, they kneel before George (now with a red sash, far right) as he holds a pan of water, baptizing them.

In the last panel (right wall), St. Augustine pauses while writing. He hears something. The dog hears it, too. It's the encouraging voice of St. Jerome, echoing mysteriously through the spacious room.

▶ *€5. Open Mon 13:30-17:30, Tue-Sat 9:30-17:30, Sun 9:30-13:30, on Calle dei Furlani at Castello 3259a, tel. 041-522-8828.*

The Scuola is located midway between St. Mark's Square and the Arsenale. Go north from Campo San Provolo (by the Church of San Zaccaria), following the street as it changes names from L'Osmarin to St. George to Greci. At the second bridge, turn left on Fondamenta dei Furlani.

Naval Museum, Arsenale, and Ship Pavilion

The mighty Republic of Venice was home to a state-of-the-art shipyard that used standardized parts and an assembly line. They could crank out an entire galley in a single day—and did so to intimidate visiting heads of state. While the Arsenale is still a military base and is therefore closed to the public, its massive and evocative gate—the Porta Magna, guarded by impressive stone lions—is worth a look.

The Naval Museum (Museo Storico Navale), which may be closed for restoration, is old-school and military-run, but anyone into maritime history or sailing will find its several floors of exhibits interesting. When it reopens, you'll see the evolution of warships, displays on old fishing boats, and gondolas. The Ship Pavilion (Padiglione delle Navi), open during the museum restoration, is across the Arsenale Bridge and has military vessels and ancient ceremonial gondolas.

▶ *€5, Ship Pavilion-Mon-Thu 8:45-13:00, Fri 8:45-17:00, Sat-Sun 10:00-17:00, Naval Museum-may be closed for restoration; if open, likely same hours as Ship Pavilion, shorter hours in winter, off Riva San Biasio, Castello 2148, tel. 041-244-1399, www.visitmuve.it/en/museums. From the Doge's Palace, hike six bridges east along the waterfront to the Naval Museum. To see the Arsenale gate, turn left at the museum and follow the canal.*

Murano

BRIDGES

9 MIN.
via Cimitero

Fondamente
Nove · Line12

Lines 4.1 & 4.2

Colonna

Museo

Cimitero

Faro

San
Michele

See Murano detail
map below

Venice

Line 12   30-40 MIN.

Lagoon

Murano

200 Meters

200 Yards

SANTA MARIA
DEGLI ANGELI

F. SEBASTIANO VENIER

Lagoon

Serenella

RAMO
DI
MULA

Venier

Da
Mula

LA MURINA
GLASS SHOP

GLASS
MUSEUM

F. CASE NOVE

SAN PIETRO
MARTIRE

SAN MARIA E
SAN DONATO

Colonna
Lines
4.1 & 4.2

MALL &
SUPER-
MARKET

VENINI
GLASS
SHOP

FIRE
TOWER

RIVA LONGA

To San Michele
& Venice

FONDAMENTA DEI VETRAI

F. DAN. MANIN

BRESSAGIO

FARO

Museo

F. ANDREA NAVAGERO

AI DOGI
GLASS
DEMO

Faro

LIGHT-
HOUSE

Navagero

To Venice

Line 12

To
Burano

Lagoon Tour

1 Kilometer

1 Mile

Lagoon

10-MIN. WALK

SANTA MARIA ASSUNTA

San Giacomo

Laghi

Mazzorbo

Torcello
Line 12
5 MIN.

See Burano detail map below

V *Burano*

Burano

Lines 12 & 14

⌢ Bridges

Burano

Mazzorbo
Line 12

To Torcello

To Murano

Torcello

Line 12

COMARE

SAN MAURO

Line 12 & 14

MARCELLO

F. S. MAURO

To Treporti, Punta Sabbioni & (#14) Lido & San Zaccaria

Lagoon

VIA B. GALUPPI

C. PITTONA

FONDAMENTA DE LA GIUDECCA

DEL PIZZO

FISH MARKET

WC

Piazza Galuppi

LACE MUSEUM

VIGNA

F. TERANOVA

POST

San Martino Church & Leaning Bell Tower

Park

100 Meters

100 Yards

SIGHTS

La Biennale

Every year (June-Nov), the city hosts a world's fair of art—contemporary visual art in odd years and architecture in even years. Representatives from many nations show off the latest trends, housed in buildings and pavilions scattered throughout Giardini park and the Arsenale.

▶ *Take vaporetto #1 or #2 to Giardini-Biennale. See the events calendar at www.labiennale.org.*

Sant'Elena

This 100-year-old suburb at the tip of the fish's tail shows a completely non-touristy, residential side of Venice. You'll find a kid-friendly park, a few lazy restaurants, and beautiful sunsets over San Marco.

▶ *Walk, or catch vaporetto #1 from St. Mark's Square to Sant'Elena.*

Lagoon Tour

North of the city are four islands easily laced together in a pleasant day trip. They sit in Venice's lagoon, a calm section of the Adriatic protected from wind and waves by the natural breakwater of the Lido. The islands offer an escape from the crowds, a chance to get out on a boat, and some enjoyable diversions for fans of glassmaking and lace.

Here they are, from nearest to farthest:

San Michele (at the Cimitero stop on the way to Murano) is the cemetery island—the final resting place of Venetians and a few foreign VIPs, from poet Ezra Pound to composer Igor Stravinsky.

▲**Murano,** where glass has been made since the 1200s, has several glass factories giving glass-blowing demonstrations, and the Glass Museum (open daily, tel. 041-739-586, http://museovetro.visitmuve.it). Besides the vaporetto, you can get to Murano from St. Mark's Square by taking a round-trip boat tour (€20, 4 hours, www.alilaguna.it) or a free ride that comes with a sales pitch. If you just want a glass-blowing demonstration without leaving St. Mark's Square, see page 196.

▲▲**Burano** is famous for lacemaking, with shops and a Lace Museum (closed Mon, tel. 041-730-034, http://museomerletto.visitmuve. it). The town itself (pop. 2,700) is a delightful pastel fishing village.

▲**Torcello,** population 20, is a marshy wasteland, home to Venice's oldest church (with a Last Judgment mosaic on the back wall), a climbable bell tower, and a modest museum (church open daily, museum closed Mon, tel. 041-730-119).

The island of Burano in the lagoon is a smaller, sleepier version of Venice.

▶ *Of the many transportation options, I suggest linking the islands with this route:*

    1. Catch vaporetto #4.1 or #4.2 to Murano-Colonna, departing from San Zaccaria (near St. Mark's, 40 minutes), or the train station (40 minutes), or Fondamente Nove (on the fish's back, 10 minutes).

    2. Continue on from Murano-Faro to Burano, on vaporetto #12 (30-40 minutes).

    3. From Burano, take #12 to Torcello (5 minutes).

    4. Return home from Burano on the #12 to Fondamente Nove (45 minutes).

Lido Beach

Venice's nearest beach is the Lido, across the lagoon on an island connected to the mainland (which means car traffic). It's sandy, family-friendly, and good for swimming, with umbrellas, beach gear, and food available.

▶ *Take vaporetto: Lido S.M.E., then walk 10 minutes on Gran Viale S. Maria Elisabetta to beach entry.*

Sleeping

Choosing the right neighborhood in Venice is as important as choosing the right hotel. For sheer magic, I favor hotels that may be a bit pricier but are close to the action: near St. Mark's, Rialto, and the quaint Accademia/Dorsoduro area. I also list a few hotels near the train station (less charming but handy for train travelers). I like hotels that are clean, central, relatively quiet at night (except for the singing of gondoliers), traditional, family-run, and friendly.

Double rooms listed in this book will range from €90 (very simple, with toilet and shower down the hall) to €400 (plush Grand Canal views and maximum plumbing), with most clustered around €140-180 (with private bathrooms). As many hotels in central Venice are in historic buildings, rooms tend to be small and stairs are often plentiful.

Unless noted, these listings come without an elevator. If that's a concern, request a room on a lower floor.

I rank accommodations from **$** budget to **$$$$** splurge (see sidebar). Venice levies a tax on hotel rooms. This tax is generally not included in the prices in this book, and must be paid in cash at checkout. It varies from €1 to €4 per person, per night, depending on how many stars the hotel has.

A Typical Venice Hotel

A €150 double room in Venice is small by American standards and has one double bed or two twins and a private bathroom with a toilet, sink, and bathtub or shower. Rooms generally have a telephone and TV, and may have a safe. Most hotels at this price will have air-conditioning—cheaper places may not. Some rooms have a small fridge stocked with drinks for sale. In Venice, a canalside room sounds romantic, but in reality you might be sleeping next to a busy, noisy, boat- and gondola-clogged "street." The quietest Venetian rooms will probably face a courtyard.

Breakfast is generally included. It's usually a self-service buffet of bread, ham, cheese, yogurt, and juice, while a server takes your coffee order.

Nearly all hotels have some form of Internet access, likely free or with a small charge. The staff speaks at least enough English to get by. Night clerks aren't paid enough to care deeply about problems that arise.

Making Reservations

Reserve your rooms as soon as you've pinned down your travel dates, especially if you'll be traveling during peak season (April-June and Sept-Oct). For busy national holidays, it's wise to reserve far in advance (see page 186). For family-run hotels, it's generally cheaper to book your room directly via email or a phone call—not on a website. For business-class hotels, or if you'd rather book online, reserve directly through the hotel's official website (not a booking agency's site). For complicated requests, send an email that covers:

- the size of your party and type of rooms you need
- your arrival and departure dates, written European-style—day followed by month and year (for example, 18/06/19 or 18 June 2019); include the total number of nights

Hotel Price Code

$$$$	**Splurge:** Most rooms over €170
$$$	**Pricier:** €130–170
$$	**Moderate:** €90–130
$	**Budget:** €50–90
¢	**Backpacker:** Under €50

These rates are for a standard double room with breakfast in high season. For the best prices, book direct.

- special requests (such as en suite bathroom vs. down the hall, cheapest room, twin beds vs. double bed, quiet room)
- applicable discounts (such as a Rick Steves reader discount, cash discount, or promotional rate)

Most places will request a credit-card number to hold your room. If you're using an online reservation form, look for the https or a lock icon at the top of your browser. If you book direct, you can email, call, or fax this information. Always call or email to reconfirm your room reservation a few days in advance. If you must cancel your reservation, it's polite to do so with as much notice as possible. Cancellation policies can be strict; read the fine print or ask about these before you book.

Because finding addresses is tricky in Venice, get clear directions to the hotel from the hotelier or their website. Let them know your arrival point in Venice (e.g., the train station, or the airport) and they can suggest the best mode of transportation and walking directions. Alternatively, at www.venicexplorer.net you can find your hotel on a map, if you know the district and address number (click "Venice Civic Number" to start).

Budget Tips

To get the best deal, contact my family-run hotels directly by phone or email. By going direct, the owners avoid a roughly 20 percent commission imposed by booking services, giving them wiggle room to offer you a discount, a nicer room, or free breakfast if it's not already included. In addition, some of my listed hotels offer special rates to my readers—it's worth asking when you book your room.

Due to supply outstripping demand, Venetian hotel rates can be surprisingly soft, and you can get deals below the quoted rate. To get the best rates at business-class hotels, start with the hotel's website, looking for promo deals. Check rates every few days, as prices can vary greatly based on demand. Email several hotels to ask for their best price and compare offers—you may be astonished at the range. You may get a better rate if you offer to pay cash, stay at least three nights, skip breakfast, or simply ask if there are any cheaper rooms. There are fewer bargains during peak season. But rates can drop dramatically (50 percent) off-season—roughly November through March and in July and August.

Big, expensive hotels are most likely to mark down rooms. Try Hotel Giorgione (www.hotelgiorgione.com); Casa Verardo (www.casaverardo.it); or Hotel all'Angelo. Hotel Donà Palace, Hotel al Ponte dei Sospiri—three sister hotels (www.carrainhotelsgroup.com) and Ca' Dei Conti (www.cadeiconti.com) are also good options.

In addition to hotels, I also list a few alternatives: bed-and-breakfasts (B&Bs); hostels (for more listings see www.hostelworld.com or www.hihostels.com); and church-run places with good prices in an institutional, twin-bed setting. Airbnb.com makes it reasonably easy to find a place to sleep in someone's home.

Don't be too cheap when picking a hotel in Venice. Having a nice place to call home is part of the romance of this romantic city.

NEAR ST. MARK'S SQUARE
Central as can be, near sights, shops, restaurants, and handy vaporetto stop San Zaccaria

$$$$ Hotel Flora San Marco 2283a, on Calle Bergamaschi tel. 041-520-5844 www.hotelflora.it	West of St. Mark's, amid fashion boutiques on Grand Canal, formal uniformed staff but homey warm oasis
$$$$ Hotel Mercurio San Marco 1848, on Calle del Fruttariol tel. 041-522-0947 www.hotelmercurio.com	Near La Fenice, 29 peaceful, comfortable rooms, canal view extra
$$$$ Hotel Campiello Castello 4647, steps from San Zaccaria vaporetto stop	tel. 041-520-5764 www.hcampiello.it	East of the square, ideal location, tranquil, lacy and bright, family-run professional refuge, apartment available
$$$$ Hotel Fontana Castello 4701, on Campo San Provolo tel. 041-522-0579 www.hotelfontana.it	Pleasant, family-run, overlooking lively square, two bridges behind St. Mark's, terrace rooms extra
$$$$ Locanda al Leon Castello 4270, just off Campo Santi Filippo e Giacomo	tel. 041-277-0393 www.hotelalleon.com	Feels a little like a medieval tower house, conscientiously run
$$$$ Hotel Orion Calle Spadaria 700a, 10 steps toward St. Mark's from San Zulian Church tel. 041-522-3053 www.hotelorion.it	Peaceful, simple, welcoming rooms high above touristy street, steep stairs, 2 minutes inland from square
$$$ Locanda Silva Castello 4423, on Fondamenta del Remedio	tel. 041-522-7643 www.locandasilva.it	Well-located, functional 1960s-era hotel, simple rooms, good location
$$$ Locanda Casa Querini Castello 4388, on Campo San Zaninovo/ Giovanni Novo	tel. 041-241-1294 www.locandaquerini.com	Bright, high-ceilinged rooms tucked away behind St. Mark's, enjoy sunny breakfast on the quiet square
$$$ Hotel al Piave Castello 4838, on Rua Giuffa tel. 041-528-5174 www.hotelalpiave.com	North of St. Mark's; fresh, modern, comfortable rooms above bright, tight lobby; nice neighborhood

$$ Albergo Doni Castello 4656, on Fondamenta del Vin tel. 041-522-4267 www.albergodoni.it	Dark and quiet, well-worn once-classy rooms up a creaky stairway, friendly owners, cheaper rooms with shared bath, overflow apartments available
$$ Corte Campana B&B Castello 4410, on Calle del Remedio tel. 041-523-3603, mobile 389-272-6500 www.cortecampana.com	Enthusiastic owner, three quiet characteristic rooms (one with bath down hall), lots of stairs, behind St. Mark's, cash only
$ Casa per Ferie Santa Maria della Pietà Castello 3701, 100 yards from San Zaccaria-Pietà vaporetto dock, down Calle de la Pietà from La Pietà Church tel. 041-244-3639 www.bedandvenice.it	Dorm-style rooms (formerly church-run) with 53 beds in 15 rooms, bathroom down hall, public lagoon-view terrace

RIALTO BRIDGE
Choose the busy east side of the bridge (10-minute walk to St. Mark's) or less-touristy west side, good vaporetto connections

$$$$ Hotel al Ponte Antico Cannaregio 5768, 100 yards north of bridge tel. 041-241-1944 www.alponteantico.com	Professional yet romantic, plush rooms, velvety public spaces, pricey Grand Canal views, better value in back
$$$ Pensione Guerrato San Polo 240a, on Calle drio la Scimia tel. 041-528-5927 www.hotelguerrato.com	West of bridge, 800-year-old building near colorful market; simple, spacious, airy rooms; friendly owners, apartments available
$$$ Locanda la Corte Castello 6317, on Calle Bressanatel tel. 041-241-1300 www.locandalacorte.it	Perfumed with elegance but not snooty, attractive wood-beamed pastel rooms circling quiet courtyard, some suites
$$$ Hotel al Ponte Mocenigo Santa Croce 1985 tel. 041-524-4797 www.alpontemocenigo.com	16th-century Venetian palazzo, 10-minute walk northeast of Rialto Bridge, garden terrace, great value

ACCADEMIA/DORSODURO
Quiet ambience, art galleries, convenient vaporetto stops (Accademia or Zattere)

$$$$ Pensione Accademia Dorsoduro 1058, on Fondamenta Bollani tel. 041-521-0188 www.pensioneaccademia.it	Aristocratic old palazzo with comfortable, elegant rooms, grand public spaces, and wistful breezy gardens; no elevator but few stairs
$$$$ Hotel Belle Arti Dorsoduro 912a, 100 yards behind Accademia museum | tel. 041-522-6230 www.hotelbellearti.com	Pricey, formal stern staff, lacks personality but has inviting garden terrace
$$$$ Novecento Hotel San Marco 2683, on Calle del Dose, off Campo San Maurizio | tel. 041-241-3765 www.novecento.biz	North of Accademia Bridge, tasteful boutique hotel, plush rooms, big and elegant public spaces, lots of stairs
$$$$ Hotel la Calcina Dorsoduro 780, near Zattere vaporetto stop at south end of Rio de San Vio tel. 041-520-6466 www.lacalcina.com	Formal, professional, three-star comfort; intimate, nautical-feeling rooms are squeaky clean; peaceful canalside setting, view terrace, lots of stairs and no elevator
$$$$ Don Orione Religious Guest House Dorsoduro 909a, on Rio Terà A. Foscarini tel. 041-522-4077 www.donorione-venezia.it	Big institution, like a modern retreat center, clean, peaceful, comfortable, strictly run, fine value
$$$$ Casa Rezzonico Dorsoduro 2813, near Ca' Rezzonico vaporetto stop on Fondamenta Gherardini tel. 041-277-0653 www.casarezzonico.it	Tranquil getaway far from crowds, seven inviting rooms, grassy private garden terrace
$$$$ Hotel Galleria Dorsoduro 878a, 30 yards from Accademia museum | tel. 041-523-2489 www.hotelgalleria.it	Narrow velvety rooms, most with views of Grand Canal, family-run, no air-con but fans

$$$ Foresteria Levi San Marco 2893, on Calle Giustinian just north of Accademia Bridge tel. 041-277-0542 www.foresterialevi.it	Foundation-run; quiet, comfortable, spacious yet institutional rooms; some loft quads available, prices vary wildly
$$$ Istituto Ciliota San Marco 2976, on Calle de le Muneghe just off Campo San Stefano, north of Accademia Bridge | tel. 041-520-4888 www.ciliota.it	Big, well-run, sparkling-clean institution with dorm-like rooms, industrial-strength comfort, little character but good value
$$$ Casa di Sara Dorsoduro 1330, along Fondamenta de le Romite | tel. 342-596-3563 www.casadisara.com	Colorfully decorated little B&B, maximum privacy hidden on quiet leafy back street, tiny roof terrace
¢ Venice's Youth Hostel Fondamenta Zitelle 86, from Zitelle vaporetto stop, walk right along the embankment | tel. 041-523-8211 www.hostelvenice.org	On Giudecca Island south of Dorsoduro, 243 bunk beds in dorm rooms, private rooms available, full facilities, grand views, great deal for backpackers
NEAR THE TRAIN STATION **It's charmless, but if you must stay here, these places stand out**	
$$$$ Hotel Abbazia Cannaregio 68, 2 blocks from station on quiet Calle Priuli dei Cavaletti tel. 041-717-333 www.abbaziahotel.com	Big former abbey has history and class, grand living room and garden, fun staff, lots of stairs
$$$ Locanda Ca' San Marcuola Cannaregio 1763, near San Marcuola vaporetto stop | tel. 041-716-048 www.casanmarcuola.com	Peaceful, characteristic oldie-but-goodie, 14 fine rooms, some canal views, good value
$$$ Locanda Herion Cannaregio 1697a, on Campiello Augusto Picutti | tel. 041-275-9426 www.locandaherion.com	13 beige-tiled, homey rooms, on sleepy lane just off a busy shopping street near San Marcuola vaporetto
$$ Hotel Henry Cannaregio 1506e, on Calle Ormesini at Campiello Briani | tel. 041-523-6675 www.hotelhenry.it	15 simple, flowery rooms near Jewish Ghetto, small and family-owned, no public spaces, no breakfast

Eating

Venetians enjoy some of the best seafood and greatest dining ambience in the world. Lingering over a multicourse meal with loved ones while you sip wine and watch the play of light on the water...it's one of Venice's great pleasures.

On the other hand, Venetian restaurants are inevitably touristy (no restaurant can survive on locals alone) and pricey (since all produce must be shipped in). But Venice offers dining experiences found nowhere else in Italy.

I list a full range of restaurants and eateries—from budget options for a quick bite to multicourse splurges with maximum ambience. I prefer mom-and-pop, personality-driven places, offering fine value and high quality with a local reputation.

When in Venice, I eat on the Venetian schedule. For breakfast, I

Restaurant Price Code

I've assigned each eatery a price category, based on the average cost of a typical main course (pasta or *secondi*). Drinks, desserts, and splurge items (steak and seafood) can raise the price considerably.

$$$$	**Splurge:** Most main courses over €20
$$$	**Pricier:** €15-20
$$	**Moderate:** €10-15
$	**Budget:** Under €10

In Italy, pizza by the slice and other takeaway food is **$**; a basic trattoria or sit-down pizzeria is **$$**; a casual but more upscale restaurant is **$$$**; and a swanky splurge is **$$$$**. The circled numbers in the restaurant listings indicate locations on the maps on pages 171-177.

eat at the hotel or grab a pastry and cappuccino at the neighborhood bar. Lunch is fast and simple to make time for sightseeing—a sandwich in a bar (as locals do), a slice of pizza, or a self-service cafeteria. Evening time is for drinks and appetizers in a *cicchetti* bar, or for slowing down and savoring a full restaurant meal.

Restaurants

Restaurants generally serve lunch from about 12:00 to 15:00. Dinner is served to Venetians after 21:00 and to tourists at 19:00 (quality restaurants rarely open much earlier). Reservations are not always necessary but can be smart, especially on busy weekends.

Get used to the reality that most restaurants (even my recommendations) are frequented by fellow tourists. Minimize the tourist hordes by eating later, by avoiding triple-language-menu places and laminated pictures of food, or by escaping to the less-touristed Dorsoduro area. Choose between romantic canalside ambience with overpriced food, or hole-in-the-wall places with a local clientele—it's hard to get both.

A full restaurant meal comes in courses: appetizer (*antipasto*), a plate of pasta, meat or seafood course (*secondo*), salad, dessert, coffee, liqueurs, and so on. It can take hours, and the bill can add up quickly, so plan your strategy before sitting down to a restaurant meal.

For light eaters, there's nothing wrong with ordering a single dish as your meal—a plate of pasta, an antipasto, or a salad. Ordering an individual-size pizza and a carafe of wine can buy you a great canal-side setting for a reasonable price. Couples could each order a dish (or two) and share. If you want a full meal at a predictable price, consider the *menu turistico*—a fixed-price multicourse meal where you can choose from a list of menu items. It includes the service charge, and is usually a good value for non-gourmets.

In Venice, only rude waiters rush you. For speedier service, be prepared with your next request whenever a waiter happens to grace your table. You'll have to ask for the bill—mime-scribble on your raised palm or ask, *"Il conto, per favore?"*

Quick Budget Meals

Venice offers many budget options for hungry travelers.

Italian "bars" are cafés, not taverns. These neighborhood hang-outs serve coffee, sandwiches (grilled *panini* or cold *tramezzini*), mini pizzas, premade salads, fresh-squeezed orange juice (*spremuta*), and drinks from the cooler.

Various cafeteria-style places dish out fast and cheap cooked meals to eat there or take out. You can buy pizza by the slice at little hole-in-the-wall places, sold by weight (100 grams for a small slice). Ethnic joints serve Turkish *döner kebabs* (meat and veggies wrapped in pita bread). *Cicchetti* bars (see next page) serve small build-a-meal toothpick snacks for the local crowd at lunch and in the evening.

At any eating establishment (however humble), be aware that the price of your food and drink may be 20-40 percent more if you consume it while sitting at a table instead of standing at the bar. This two-tier price system will always be clearly posted. Don't sit without first checking out the financial consequences. Also, at many bars, the custom is to first pay the cashier for what you want, then hand the receipt to a barista who serves you. Because Venice has so few public places to sit and relax, it can be worth a few extra euros to enjoy your coffee, sandwich, or gelato while seated in an air-conditioned café.

Venice is not a great town for picnics. The city prohibits picnics in most public spaces, so don't sit down and spread out a lavish feast in a highly touristed area. But even locals grab a sandwich or slice of pizza "to go" (*da portar via*) and eat discreetly outside the tourist zone. Buy some fruit, refill your water bottle at a public tap...and dine like a doge. The Rialto Market (west end of the bridge) is a picnic-buyer's paradise. Hole-in-the-wall grocery stores (*alimentari*) can be hard to find in the tourist zones. There's a produce stand 100 yards behind St. Mark's Basilica, just north of Campo Santi Filippo e Giacomo. When buying produce, it's customary to let the merchant pick it out. If something is a mystery, ask for a small taste (*"Un assaggio, per favore?"*).

Cicchetti Pubs

Pubs (*bacari*) are a big part of the Venetian scene. Locals stop in at lunch or early evening for a drink and to snack on various finger foods (*cicchetti*). The foods range from cheese to olives to deep-fried artichokes to crostini to calamari to anything ugly on a toothpick. It's easy to build a meal out of small €2-3 servings. Or get an assortment (*un piatto di misti*) for around €8. Just belly up to the bar, point to the *cicchetti* you want (it's displayed on trays), and eat, either standing or sitting at a table—for *cicchetti,* the cost is usually the same. Many pubs also serve pastas and meat dishes.

For drinks, you'll find a variety of wines by the glass (*un ombra* for as little as €1). The dominant pre-dinner drink (*aperitivo*) is a white-wine-and-spirits cocktail called a spritz. A *spritz con Compari* is bitter; a *spritz con Aperol* is sweeter. Another Venetian specialty is a sparkling, peach-flavored Bellini.

Bars don't stay open very late, the food selection is best from about 18:00 to 20:00, and most places are closed Sunday. To do a pub crawl (*giro d'ombra*), there's a great area west of the Rialto Bridge (see the "*Cicchetti* Strip" listing, page 165). Come ready to mingle. Boldly order a Bellini, a *spritz con Aperol,* or a prosecco, and draw approving looks from the natives.

Venetian Cuisine

Along with the basic dishes you'll find all over Italy, Venice has its signature specialties—mainly, a wide variety of catch-of-the-day seafood. Venetian cuisine relies heavily on fish, shellfish, risotto, and polenta.

For appetizers, try a marinated seafood assortment (*antipasto di mare*) or asiago cheese. Risotto (rice simmered in broth) and polenta (grilled cornmeal porridge) are more traditional than pasta. Seafood is the classic main dish. The more exotic it is, the more local: fish (generally smaller varieties like sardines, not salmon or trout), shellfish, octopus, eel, weird crustaceans, and cuttlefish (*seppia*). Seafood is often sold expensively by the gram—confirm the total price before ordering. On a menu, "x2" means the price per person for a large, two-person dish.

No meal in Italy is complete without wine. Even the basic house wine (*vino da tavola* or *vino della casa*) is fine with a meal. The island of Venice produces no wine, but the mainland Veneto region is known for Soave (crisp white, great with seafood), Valpolicella (light fruity red), Amarone (very intense red), and prosecco (a dry sparkling wine, easy to drink too much).

Italian coffee is some of the world's best. Even the most basic hole-in-the-wall bar serves quality espresso, macchiatos, and cappuccinos. Popular liqueurs to finish a meal are *amaro* (various brands) and anise-flavored Sambuca. Venetians love dipping Burano biscotti in *fragolino,* a strawberry dessert wine. Or pick up a cup or cone of gelato at a gelateria and stroll the streets with the rest of Venice, enjoying a bit of edible art.

EATING

RIALTO
North of the Rialto Bridge, near the Strada Nova (see map, pages 170-171)

❶	**$$$ Trattoria da Bepi** Cannaregio 4550, half a block off Campo Santi Apostoli on Salizada Pistor tel. 041-528-5031	Bright and alpine-paneled, traditional cuisine, sit inside or out, trust owner's seafood recommendations (Fri-Wed 12:00-14:30 & 19:00-22:00, closed Thu)
❷	**$$$ La Cantina** Cannaregio 3689, facing Campo San Felice on Strada Nova near Ca' d'Oro tel. 041-522-8258	Rustic yet sophisticated wine bar serving cold meat, cheese, fish plates, and *cicchetti*; not cheap but good people-watching (Mon-Sat 11:00-22:00, closed Sun)
❸	**$$$$ Vini da Gigio** Cannaregio 3628a, behind the church on Campo San Felice tel. 041-528-5140	Small place with big enthusiasm for traditional food (Wed-Sun 12:00-14:30 & 19:00-22:30, closed Mon-Tue)

RIALTO
East end of the Rialto Bridge (see map, pages 170-171)

❹	**$$$ Osteria al Mascaron** Castello 5225, on Calle Lunga Santa Maria Formosa, a block past Campo Santa Maria Formosa tel. 041-522-5995	Rustic bar-turned-restaurant serving sumptuous pastas with steamy seafood, €16 antipasto misti plate makes a terrific light meal (Mon-Sat 12:00-15:00 & 19:00-23:00, closed Sun)
❺	**$ Rosticceria Gislon** San Marco 5424, through the covered passageway near the statue on Campo San Bartolomeo tel. 041-522-3569	Cheap self-service diner for takeout or eat in (but skip their restaurant upstairs), surly staff (daily 9:00-21:30)
❻	**$$ Osteria al Portego** Castello 6015, on Calle de la Malvasia tel. 041-522-9038	Friendly neighborhood eatery, fine meals at tables (reserve) or *cicchetti* at bar (daily 12:00-14:30 & 17:30-21:30)
❼	**$$$$ Osteria alle Testiere** Castello 5801, on Calle del Mondo Novo just off Campo Santa Maria Formosa tel. 041-522-7220	My top dining splurge in Venice for creative seafood, budget €50 and trust your host, mandatory reservations by email only to info@osteriallestestiere (closed Sun-Mon)

RIALTO
West end of the Rialto Bridge (see map, pages 170-171)

8	**$$-$$$ The "Bancogiro Stretch"** Along Grand Canal near the Rialto Market	Several eateries with seating along Grand Canal; serving lunch, between-meal bar snacks, dinner, or late drinks with a youthful crowd; great for a spritz and *cicchetti* (long hours daily)
9	**$ The "*Cicchetti* Strip"** Along Sotoportego dei Do Mori and Calle de le Do Spade	Classic bars serving *cicchetti* (and some meals) two blocks inland from Rialto Market—look for Cantina Do Spade, Osteria ai Storti, Bar all'Arco, and Cantina Do Mori (long hours daily)
10	**$ Al Mercà** San Polo 213, on Campo Cesare Battisti	Lively nook (no tables) with happy local crowd, light fare, tourists don't faze them (Mon-Sat 10:00-14:30 & 18:00-21:00, closed Sun)
11	**$$$ Ristorante Vini da Pinto** San Polo 367a, on Campo de le Becarie facing fish market tel. 041-522-4599	Tourist-friendly food, good service, relaxed outdoor seating, make sure you're at the right restaurant—not their neighbors (long hours daily)
12	**$$ Osteria al Ponte Storto** San Polo 1278, down Calle Bianca from San Aponal church tel. 041-528-2144	Little place on quiet canalside corner a block off the main drag, good-value set-price meals (Tue-Sun 12:00-15:00 & 19:00-21:45, closed Mon)
13	**$$$$ Trattoria Antiche Carampane** San Polo 1911, on Rio Tera delle Carampane tel. 041-524-0165	Dressy, family-run place, open kitchen, traditional dishes with a twist, passion for fish, reservations necessary (Tue-Sat 12:45-14:30 & 19:30-22:30, closed Sun-Mon)
14	**$$ Antica Birraria la Corte** On Campo San Polo at #2168, between Rialto Bridge and Frari Church tel. 041-275-0570	Everyday eatery on family-filled square, pizza and salads, beer hall inside or outside (daily 12:00-15:00 & 18:00-22:30)
15	**$$ Osteria al Garanghelo** San Polo 1570, on Calle dei Boteri tel. 041-721-721	Happy little eatery with inviting menu, fresh fish, and old but shiny ambience, seafood tasting platter and vegetarian dishes (open daily)

EATING

⑯	**$$-$$$ Rialto Bridge Tourist Traps** Along Grand Canal near Rialto Bridge	Gauntlet of restaurants along the Grand Canal offering lousy overpriced food, aggressive waiters, lots of tourists...and stunning views—to enjoy the ambience on the cheap, order a simple pizza/pasta and drink; confirm minimum charge before you order (long hours daily)

NEAR ST. MARK'S SQUARE
In addition to the ultra-atmospheric cafés directly on the square, here are some other options nearby (see map, pages 172-173)

⑰	**$$$$ Ristorante Antica Sacrestia** Castello 4463, behind San Zaninovo/Giovanni Novo Church on Calle Corona tel. 041-523-0749	Hands-on owner, creative €35-80 fixed-price meals or à la carte in lovely setting, reasonable pizza for lunch (Tue-Sun 11:30-15:00 & 18:00-23:00, closed Mon)
⑱	**$ "Sandwich Row"** Along Calle de le Rasse, just east of St. Mark's Square, from Bridge of Sighs, head down the Riva and take second lane on the left	Several bars along Calle de le Rasse offer sandwiches, salads, and a place to sit (€1 extra); I like Birreria Forst at #4540 and Bar Verde at #4526 (most places open daily 7:00-24:00)
⑲	**$$ Ristorante alla Basilica** Castello 4255, one block behind St. Mark's Basilica on Calle dei Albanesitel. 041-522-0524	Institutional-feeling place serves a solid €16 fixed-price lunch (nothing else) and has air-con (Wed-Mon 12:00-15:00, closed Tue)
⑳	**$ Ristorante Cinese Capitol** Castello 4294, Campo S.S. Filippo e Giacomo tel. 041-522-5331	Inexpensive but tasty Chinese standards to eat in or take out (daily 11:00-15:30 & 17:30-23:00)
㉑	**$ Picnicking in Giardinetti Reali Park**	Though you can't picnic on St. Mark's Square, you can in Giardinetti Reali park, west along the waterfront.
㉒	**$$-$$$ Canalside Tourist Traps** Several blocks behind St. Mark's, on Fondamenta San Lorenzo near the Ponte dei Greci bridge	While tourist traps, Ristorante alla Conchiglia and Trattoria da Giorgio ai Greci have romantic tables by gondolier-frequented canals (long hours daily)

ACCADEMIA/DORSODURO
Near Accademia Bridge (pretty touristy), Zattere vaporetto (less touristy), and Campo San Barnaba (most charming) (see map, pages 174-175)

㉓	**$$ Bar Foscarini** Dorsoduro 878c, next to Accademia Bridge on Rio Terà A. Foscarini tel. 041-522-7281	OK pizzas and *panini,* some Grand Canal views, also serves breakfast (daily 8:00-23:00, until 20:30 Nov-April)
㉔	**$ Enoteca Cantine del Vino Già Schiavi** Dorsoduro 992, 100 yards from Accademia museum on San Trovaso canal tel. 041-523-0034	Wine shop much loved for cheap *cicchetti* and sandwiches, bottles to go (Mon-Sat 8:30-20:30, closed Sun)
㉕	**$ Bar al Maraveje** Dorsoduro 1185, 100 yards west of Accademia, just over bridge on Calle de la Toletta tel. 041-523-5768	Quiet comfy tables, fresh sandwiches (daily)
㉖	**$ Al Vecio Marangon** Dorsoduro 1210, 100 yards west of Accademia on Calle de la Toletta tel. 041-525-5768	Tight, stylishly rustic bar serves *cicchetti*-style dishes and pastas, outside seating available (daily 12:00-22:00)
㉗	**$$$ Terrazza dei Nobili** Dorsoduro 924, north of Zattere vaporetto stop tel. 041-520-6895	Enjoy a warm, romantic evening along the canal, creative specialties at tolerable prices (daily 12:00-24:00)
㉘	**$ Oke Pizzeria** Dorsoduro 1414, 250 yards west of Zattere vaporetto stop tel. 041-520-6601	Casual tables on embankment or sprawling pizza-parlor interior, youthful and fun (daily 11:30-23:00)
㉙	**$$$ Ristoteca Oniga** Dorsoduro 2852, on Campo San Barnaba tel. 041-522-4410	Accessible, fresh seafood and vegetarian options in cozy interior or at tables on the square, reservations smart (Wed-Mon 12:00-14:30 & 19:00-22:30, closed Tue in winter)
㉚	**$$$ Osteria Enoteca Ai Artisti** Dorsoduro 1169a, Fondamenta de la Toletta tel. 041-523-8944	Well-presented, small wine-snob interior or romantic canalside tables, wines by the glass (Mon-Sat 12:45-15:00 & 19:00-22:00, closed Sun)

EATING

31	**$$ Pizzeria al Profeta** Dorsoduro 2671, from Campo San Barnaba, walk down Calle Lunga San Barnaba tel. 041-523-7466	Big, casual, woody interior or leafy garden, pizza and steak, convivial atmosphere (Wed-Mon 12:00-14:30 & 19:00-23:30, closed Tue)
32	**$$$ Enoteca e Trattoria la Bitta** Dorsoduro 2753a, just off Campo San Barnaba on Calle Lunga San Barnaba tel. 041-523-0531	Tiny "slow food" bistro for serious locavores (but no fish dishes), reservations required, cash only (Mon-Sat 19:00-23:00, closed Sun)

TRAIN STATION/CANNAREGIO
Residential area northeast of the station, beyond the Jewish Ghetto; explore at sunset, then grab a bite (see map, pages 176-177)

33	**$$ Pizzeria Vesuvio** Cannaregio 1837, on Rio Terà Farsetti tel. 041-795-688	Popular neighborhood favorite, classy indoor seating and pleasant tables outside (long hours, closed Wed Oct-April)
34	**$$$ Osteria di Bentigodi** Calesele-Cannaregio 1423, across from Pizzeria Vesuvio tel. 041-822-3714	Traditional dishes with creative flair and seasonal ingredients, live music nightly, reservations smart (daily 12:00-14:30 & 19:00-23:00)
35	**$$ Enoteca Cicchetteria Do Colonne** Cannaregio 1814, on Rio Terà del Cristo tel. 041-524-0453	Local dive with loyal following, OK *cicchetti* and sandwiches, fun scene feels real (daily 10:00-21:30)
36	**$ Brek** Cannaregio 124, left from station, past the bridge along Rio Terà Lista di Spagna	Near the station, self-service cafeteria chain, efficient and cheap (daily 11:30-22:00)
37	**$$$ Osteria L'Orto dei Mori** Dorsoduro 3386 on Campo dei Mori tel. 041-524-3677	Chic, nicely presented, creative Venetian cuisine, eat in elegant modern interior or on classic neighborhood square, reservations smart (Wed-Mon 12:30-15:30 & 19:00-24:00, closed Tue)
38	**$$ Osteria Ai 40 Ladroni** Cannaregio 3253, Fondamenta de la Sensa at Calle del Capitello tel. 041-715-736	Characteristic old standby, busy ambience inside or canal tables, good seafood antipasto (Tue-Sun 12:00-14:30 & 19:00-22:15, closed Mon)

EATING

To Fondamente Nove
Vaporetto
Dock

FONDAMENTE NOVE

C. VENIER

l'Acqua Dolce

C. NUOVA

C. DEL FORNO

C. DE LA MADONA

C. PROVERBI

PRETI

CANNAREGIO

Campo de la Cason

C. MAL

SAN CANZIAN

C. WIDMANN

Rio dei Mendicanti

SANTI APOSTOLI

Rio dei Santi Apostoli

Campo San Canzian

Rio TERA

SALIZADA SAN CANZIAN

Campo Corner

MAGAZEN

BOLDÙ

Campo Santa Maria Novo

CALLE DE LA TESTA

FONDAMENTA DEI MENDICANTI

HOSPITAL

BAGATAN

MIRACOLI

SANTA MARIA DEI MIRACOLI

Rio de la Panada

CALLE LARGA GALLINA

Rio de San Gio Grisostomo

SAN GRISOSTOMO

SAN GIOVANNI GRISOSTOMO

C. CASTELI

Campo Santi Giovanni & Paolo

SANTI GIOVANNI & PAOLO (SAN ZANIPOLO)

RSEO

COIN DEP'T STORE

C. DE LA ERBE

COLLEONI STATUE

F. DANDOLO

SALIZADA S. ZANIPOLO

C. BRESSANA

MADONA

GERMAN EXCHANGE (FORMER POST)

C. SCALETA

Campo Santa Marina

Rio de Santa Marina

FRUTARIOL

C. F. FELZI

C. PIOMBO

LARGA

MARCELLO

Rio del Piombo

CASTELLO

OSPEDALETO

PISSI

WC

Campo S. Bartolomeo

5

PONTE S. ANTONIO

Rio de la Fava

C. CARMINATI

SAN LIO

C. DE LA NAVE

C. DEL DOSE

C. FOND. DEI PRETI

Rio d. Pestrin

Campo Santa Maria Formosa

C. LUNGA S. MARIA FORMOSA

4

C. DE L'AQUILA NERA

C. DEI STAGNERI

SALIZADA SAN LIO

YENIERA

DEL PARADISO

SANTA MARIA FORMOSA

C. DEI ORBI

Rio de S. M. Formosa

FAVA

Campo de la Fava

SANTA MARIA FAVA

To San Marco

MONDO NOVO

To San Marco

7

6

100 Meters

100 Yards

Restaurants near St. Mark's Square

To Rialto

SALIZADA VENIERA

Campo Santa Maria Formosa

To Rialto

CALLE LARGA SAN LORENZO

BORGOLOCO SAN LORENZO

Rio de San Lorenzo

F. SAN LORENZO

C. SAN LIO

MONDO NOVO

SANTA MARIA FORMOSA

CASTELLO

C. MALVASIA

C. SAN ANTONIO

C. PONTE DE LA GUERRA

C. DE LE BANDE

RUGA GIUFFA

C. MEZO

FOND. SAN SEVERO

Rio di San Severo

FOND. GRECI

Rio de la Guerra

San Zulian

Campo de la Guerra

SAN ZULIAN

C. DEL REMEDIO

FOND. D. REMEDIO

C. QUERINI

C. PIETRO MAGAZEN

CASTAGNA

C. DELLA CORONA

SAL. ZORZI

C. ROTTA

C. D. PRETI

22

FOND. OSMARIN

C. SPECCHIERI

C. ANZOLO

C. PIASENTINA

SAN ZANI NOVO

C. D. MERCANTI

C. DELLA CHIESA

C. SACRESTIA

San Provolo

FOND. OSMARIN

17

Rio dei Greci

MARZ. DELL' OROLOGIO

C. SPADARIA

L. SAN MARCO

C. CANONICA

C. FIGHER

Campo Santi Filippo & Giacomo

RUGA GIUFFA

C. D. MERCANTI

S. PROVOLO

Campo San Provolo

SAN ZACCARIA

Piazzetta dei Leoni

CLOCK TOWER

ST. MARK'S BASILICA

20

DIOCESAN MUSEUM

19

C. DEL ALBANESI

18

CALLE DE LE RASSE

FOND. D VIN

CORTE NUOVA

Campo San Zaccaria

TETRARCHS

CAMPANILE

PORTA DELLA CARTA

7TH COLUMN

STAIRWAY OF GIANTS

Rio de la Palazzo

BRIDGE OF SIGHS

PRISON

Rio del Vin

DEL VIN

To Public Gardens

DOGE'S PALACE

Piazzetta

PONTE DE PAGLIA

RIVA

DANIELI HOTEL

VICTOR EMMANUEL II STATUE

DEGLI

SCHIAVONI

SAN MARCO COLUMN

21

SAN THEODORE COLUMN

G

San Zaccaria-Danieli

San Zaccaria-Jolanda

San Zaccaria-M.V.E.

St. Mark's Basin

100 Meters

100 Yards

To Lido

Restaurants near Accademia/Dorsoduro

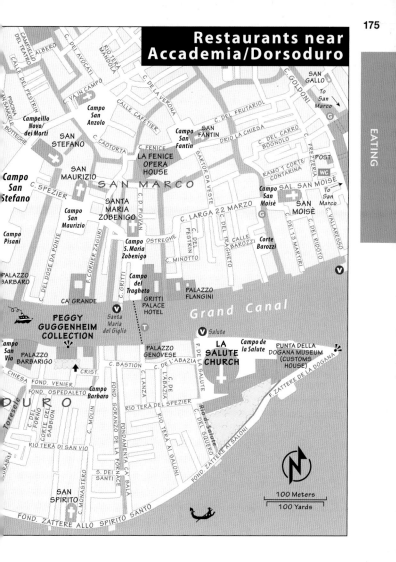

EATING

Restaurants near the Train Station/Cannaregio

SAN GIOBBE

Rio de San Giobbe

FOND. DE CANNAREGIO

C. SAN GIOVANNI

CHIOVERETE

Canale de Cannaregio

FOND PESCARIA

FOND. SAVORGNAN

C. DE LA 2 CORTI

CALLE RIELO

SAN GEREM

CALLE DELLA MISERICORDIA

100 Meters

100 Yards

N

RAMO DEI SCALZI

C. PRIULI DEI CAVALETTI

RIO. TERA LISTA DI SPAGNA

FORNO

36

SANTA LUCIA TRAIN STATION (FERROVIA)

SCALZI

i

Grand

Ferrovia W

V

Campo San Simeon Grande

CALLE PISTOR

CORTE PISANI

SCALZI BRIDGE

V

Ferrovia Scalzi

FOND. DE SAN SIMEONE PICCOLO

C. NOVA DE S. SIMEO

C. LUNGA CHIOVERETE

LIST

WC

Ferrovia

V

To Calatrava Bridge

To Piazzale Roma

SAN SIMEONE PICCOLO

Rio Marin

SAN SIMEONE GRANDE

Practicalities

PLANNING

Venice's best travel months (also its busiest and most expensive) are April, May, June, September, and October. Summer in Venice is more temperate (high 70s and 80s) than in Italy's scorching inland cities. Between November and March, expect mild winter weather (with lows in the 30s and 40s), occasional flooding, shorter sightseeing hours, cheaper hotel rates, and fewer tourists (except during the busy Carnevale festival, generally in February). March offers a good balance of low-season prices and reasonable weather.

Make sure your passport is up to date (to renew, see www.travel.state.gov). Call your debit- and credit-card companies about your plans (see below). Book hotel rooms in advance, especially for travel during peak season or holiday weekends. Consider buying travel insurance (see www.ricksteves.com/insurance). If traveling beyond Venice, research transit schedules (trains, buses) and car rentals. If renting a car, you're technically required to have an International Driving Permit (sold at your local AAA office), though I've often rented cars in Italy without one. Consider making reservations for key sights. Get a current list of museum hours at www.turismovenezia.it.

MONEY

Italy uses the euro currency: 1 euro (€) = about $1.20. To convert euros to dollars, add about 20 percent: €20 = about $24, €50 = about $60. (Check www.oanda.com for the latest exchange rates.)

Withdraw money from an ATM (known as a *bancomat* in Italy) using a debit card, just like at home. Visa and MasterCard are commonly used throughout Europe. Before departing, call your bank and credit-card company: Ask about international transaction fees, alert them that you'll be making withdrawals in Europe, and if you don't know it, get your credit card PIN. Many travelers bring a second debit/credit card as a backup. Many Italian merchants prefer cash, so withdraw large amounts (€250-300) from the ATM.

While American credit cards are accepted almost everywhere in Europe, even newer chip-style cards may not work in some payment machines (e.g., ticket kiosks). Be prepared to pay with cash, find a nearby cashier, or try entering your card's PIN.

Helpful Websites

Italian Tourist Information: www.italia.it
Venice Tourist Information: www.turismovenezia.it
Other Helpful Venice Websites: www.veneziaunica.it (vaporetto and event schedules), www.museicivicivenezianii.it (civic museums in Venice), www.venicexplorer.net (interactive maps), www.veniceforvisitors. com, www.aguestinvenice.com, and www.venicelink.com (public and private transportation tickets).
Cheap Flights: www.kayak.com (for international flights), www.sky-scanner.com (for flights within Europe)
European Train Schedules: www.bahn.com
General Travel Tips: www.ricksteves.com (helpful info on train travel, rail passes, car rental, using your mobile device, travel insurance, packing lists, and much more—plus updates to this book)

To keep your valuables safe, wear a money belt. But if you do lose your credit or debit card, report the loss immediately with a collect phone call: Visa (tel. 303/967-1096), MasterCard (tel. 636/722-7111), and American Express (tel. 336/393-1111). In Italy, to make a collect call to the US, dial 800-172-170 and stay on the line for an English-speaking operator.

ARRIVAL IN VENICE

Marco Polo Airport

Venice's small, modern airport is on the mainland shore of the lagoon, six miles north of the city (airport code: VCE). There's one sleek terminal, with a TI (daily 9:00-20:00), car-rental agencies, ATMs, a bank, and a few shops and eateries. For flight information, call 041-260-9260, visit www.veniceairport.com, or ask at your hotel.

Getting between the airport (on the mainland) and downtown Venice (on an island) can easily take two hours, so allow plenty of time. Here are your options:

Alilaguna Boats—Slow But Easy: These 50-passenger boats make the hour-plus journey between the airport dock (a short walk from the terminal) and various points in Venice. There are three key

Arrival in Venice

1 Kilometer

1 Mile

San Marco to:
Airport = 4 miles
Mestre = 5 miles
Lido = 2 miles

Lagoon

To
Padua
& Treviso
Airport

MESTRE
TRAIN STATION

Murano

Museo

CAUSEWAY

SANTA LUCIA
TRAIN
STATION

Colonna

*Guglie Grand
Bridge Canal* *Fondamenta Nove*

TRONCHETTO
CAR PARK

Tronchetto

Rialto *San Zaccaria
M.V.E.*

Marittima

PIAZZALE
ROMA
BUS STN

SAN
MARCO
San Marco

*Lido
(S.M.E.)*

MAIN
CRUISE
SHIP DOCK

Giudecca

Zattere

Zitelle

SAN
GIORGIO

Lido

----- Rail
- - - Bus
.... Alilaguna Boat
(Not all stops shown)
•–•–• People Mover

Alilaguna lines—blue, red, and orange. Some of the main stops include: San Marco, San Zaccaria (near San Marco), Rialto, Guglie (near the train station), Zattere (the Dorsoduro neighborhood), and Fondamente Nove (on the fish's back). You can reach most of this book's recommended hotels very simply by Alilaguna, with no changes. The cost is €15 (€27 round-trip, not covered by city transit passes). Boats depart roughly every 30 minutes. Get a full schedule at the TI or your hotel, call 041-240-1701, or see www.alilaguna.it.

For the trip from the airport into Venice, buy tickets inside the terminal at the TI or the Alilaguna ticket desk, or outside at the dock. To get to the boat dock, exit the arrivals hall and turn left. It's an eight-minute walk away, following signs along a paved, level, covered side-walk (easy for wheeled bags).

From Venice to the airport, boats start leaving early in the morning. Alilaguna boats can fill up, so arrive early.

Water Taxis—Fast and Direct, But Pricey: Luxury taxi speedboats zip directly between the airport and the closest dock to your hotel, getting you within steps of your destination in about 30 minutes. The official price is €110 for up to four people; add €10 for every additional person (10-passenger limit). You may get a higher quote—politely talk it down. A taxi can be a smart investment for small groups and those with an early departure.

From the airport, arrange your ride at the water-taxi desk or with the boat captains lounging at the dock (the same dock as the Alilaguna boats).

From Venice to the airport, book a day ahead, either through your hotel (easiest) or at tel. 041-522-2303 (www.motoscafivenezia.it).

Airport Shuttle Buses—Cheapest, But to Only One Destination: Buses make the 25-minute trip across the bridge from the mainland to the island, dropping you at Piazzale Roma, a major transportation hub at the "mouth of the fish." (See "Piazzale Roma Bus Station," next page.) From there, you can walk farther into Venice or catch a vaporetto down the Grand Canal. Two different, equally good bus companies (ACTV and ATVO) make the trip—just jump on whichever one's leaving next (€8 one-way, €15 round-trip, runs about 5:00-24:00, 2/hour, only 1/hour early and late, check schedules at www.atvo.it or www.actv.it). Since ACTV runs Venice's vaporetto system, they offer a discounted fare if you also buy a vaporetto pass.

From the airport to Venice, both bus companies leave from just outside the arrivals terminal. Buy tickets inside the terminal (at the TI, ticket desk, or kiosk near baggage claim), or from ticket machines at curbside. ATVO tickets are not valid on ACTV buses and vice versa. Double-check the destination; you want Piazzale Roma. If taking ACTV, you want bus #5.

From Piazzale Roma to the airport, buy your ticket from the ACTV windows or ATVO office before heading out to the platforms (although sometimes an attendant sells tickets near the buses). The newsstand in the center of the lot also sells tickets.

Santa Lucia Train Station

Venice's train station (*Venezia S.L.*) is located at the head of the Grand Canal, an easy vaporetto ride or fascinating 45-minute walk to St. Mark's Square. (Don't confuse Santa Lucia station—called "Venezia S.L."—with Venezia Mestre on the mainland.)

Minimize your time in the often-crowded station. Baggage check is at track 1. Pay WCs are also at track 1. You'll find the TI across from track 2. If you need train tickets or seat reservations (required for many Venice-Florence-Rome trains, even with a rail pass) consider doing it online or at a travel agency: Try **Agenzie 365** in the main lobby of the train station (9 percent surcharge on train tickets, tel. 041-275-9412).

The Ferrovia vaporetto stop is right outside the station's front door—vaporetto #1 (slow boat down the Grand Canal, with many stops) or vaporetto #2 (express). A water taxi into central Venice is about €60-80.

Piazzale Roma Bus Station

This open-air parking lot, located at the head of the Grand Canal, serves as a transportation hub for buses, vaporettos, cars, and the People Mover monorail. The square is a jumble of different operators, platforms, and crosswalks over busy lanes of traffic.

Get oriented. The modern Calatrava Bridge leads to the train station, a five-minute walk away. The vaporetto dock is just left of the modern bridge, where vaporetto #1 (slow) or #2 (fast) can take you down the Grand Canal to San Marco. The ACTV bus (including #5 to Marco Polo Airport) has a ticket window between the bridge and vaporetto stop. The ATVO bus ticket office (also to the airport) is at #497g in the big, white building. Also on the square are two big parking garages and the People Mover monorail to the cruise port and Tronchetto parking lot. A pay baggage-storage office is next to the monorail at #497m.

Parking Garages

The freeway dead-ends after crossing the causeway to the traffic-free island of Venice. At the end of the road you have two parking-garage choices: Tronchetto or Piazzale Roma. As you approach, signs tell you which lots are full.

Tronchetto garage is a bit farther out, a bit cheaper, and well-connected by vaporetto (€21/24 hours, tel. 041-520-7555, www.

veniceparking.it). There's little else at Tronchetto besides the helpful VèneziaUnica public transport office, aggressive salesmen, and travel agencies masquerading as TIs.

To get into downtown Venice, the easiest and cheapest way is by vaporetto #2. To find the dock, exit the garage, cross the street, and walk to the right, looking for *ACTV* signs. Line 2 has two different routes to San Marco: down the Grand Canal (more scenic, stops at Rialto, 40 minutes to San Marco), or via Giudecca (around the city, faster, no Rialto stop, 30 minutes to San Marco). A water taxi to San Marco (you'll be approached by boatmen) costs around €100. The People Mover monorail—a long walk from the parking garage—can zip you to Piazzale Roma (buy €1.50 monorail tickets with cash or a credit card from a machine).

Piazzale Roma's two garages are closer to the center of town and have more transportation options, but they're more expensive and likelier to be full. The big white Autorimessa Communale garage on the right is cheapest (€26/24 hours, tel. 041-272-7211, www.avmspa.it). The other is Garage San Marco (€32/24 hours, tel. 041-523-2213, www.garagesanmarco.it). At either garage, you'll have to give up your keys.

Cruise Ports

Most cruise ships visiting Venice dock at Stazione Marittima, located in the jaw of the fish's mouth. There's a good map of Venice's port area at www.vtp.it.

To get to St. Mark's Square, catch the Alilaguna express boat—it takes just 30 minutes. Get more info at www.alilaguna.it. The People Mover monorail to Piazzale Roma is a five-minute walk inland from the port (you'll see its elevated platform). A water taxi to anywhere in town costs around €70-80.

HELPFUL HINTS

Tourist Information (TI): Venice's crowded TIs try to help, but they're understaffed and have few free printed materials to hand out. To check or confirm something, try phoning the TI information line at 041-2424, or visit www.veneziaunica.it or www.turismovenezia.it.

If you must visit a TI, you'll find offices at the train station (daily

7:00-21:00), on St. Mark's Square (daily 9:00-19:00, in far-left corner with your back to the basilica), next to the bus station (inside the huge white parking-garage building, daily 7:30-19:30), and at the airport (daily 9:00-20:00).

Hurdling the Language Barrier: Many Italians—especially those in the tourist trade and in big cities—speak English. Still, learn the pleasantries such as *buon giorno* (good day), *mi scusi* (pardon me), *per favore* (please), *grazie* (thank you), and *arrivederci* (goodbye). For more Italian survival phrases, see page 201.

Time Zones: Italy is generally six/nine hours ahead of the East/West Coasts of the US.

Business Hours: Most businesses are open throughout the day Monday through Saturday, generally 10:00-19:00 (a bit longer in tourist areas). Though many stores close on Sunday, you'll find more open here than anywhere else in Italy. Hours can vary widely from store to store. Some small businesses close for lunch (roughly 13:00-15:30). Banking hours are generally Monday through Friday 8:30-13:30 and 15:30-16:30.

Watt's Up? Europe's electrical system is 220 volts, instead of North America's 110 volts. You'll need an adapter plug with two round prongs, sold inexpensively at travel stores in the US. Most newer electronics (such as mobile devices, laptops, hair dryers, and battery chargers) convert automatically, so you won't need a separate converter.

Numbers and Stumblers: What Americans call the second floor of a building is the first floor in Europe. Europeans write dates as day/month/year, so Christmas is 25/12/19. Commas are decimal points and vice versa—a dollar and a half is $1,50, and there are 5.280 feet in a mile.

Italy uses the metric system: A kilogram is 2.2 pounds; a liter is about a quart; and a kilometer is six-tenths of a mile. Temperature is measured in Celsius. 0°C = 32°F. To roughly convert Celsius to Fahrenheit, double the number and add 30.

Holidays: Many sights and banks close down on national holidays (though Venice stays open more than most Italian cities). Verify dates at www.italia.it or www.turismovenezia.it, or check www.ricksteves.com/festivals.

Sestieri and Addresses: Venice is divided into six districts (*sestieri*): San Marco (from St. Mark's Square to the Accademia Bridge),

Tipping

Tipping in Europe isn't as automatic and generous as it is in the US. At Italian restaurants that have waitstaff, a "service" charge (*servizio*) of about 10 percent is usually included in your bill. Some Italians don't tip beyond this, but you can add an additional tip, if you choose, by including €1-2 for each person in your party. At hotels, it's polite to give porters a euro for each bag (another reason to pack light). If you like to tip maids, leave a euro per night in your room at the end of your stay.

Castello (the area east of St. Mark's Square), Dorsoduro (the belly of the fish, on the far side the Accademia Bridge), Cannaregio (between the train station and the Rialto Bridge), San Polo (west of the Rialto Bridge), and Santa Croce (the "eye" of the fish, across the canal from the train station).

Most addresses (e.g., "Santa Croce 665b") list only the district and house number—not the street. This makes it confusing to find a specific address, so get as much information as you can. For example, the full address for Hotel Guerrato is: Calle Drio La Scimia (the street), 240/a (house number), Rialto (nearest landmark), San Polo (district).

Bookstores: The small Libreria Studium, a block behind St. Mark's Basilica, has new English books, including my guidebooks (Mon-Sat 9:00-19:30, shorter hours Sun, at Calle de la Canonica #337, tel. 041-522-2382). The funky Acqua Alta ("high water") used bookstore has prepared for the next flood by shelving its wares in bathtubs and a gondola (daily 9:00-20:00, just beyond Campo Santa Maria Formosa on Lunga Santa Maria Formosa, Castello 5176, tel. 041-296-0841).

Laundry: The coin-operated "Orange" launderette is across the Grand Canal from the train station on Ramo de le Chioverete at Santa Croce 665b (daily 7:30-22:30). For a full-service laundry (drop off and pick up two hours later), Lavanderia Gabriella is a few streets north of St. Mark's Square on Rio Terà de le Colonne at San Marco 985 (Mon-Fri 8:00-12:30, tel. 041-522-1758).

Free Water: Carry a water bottle to refill at public fountains fed by pure, tasty water piped in from the (surprisingly close) Alps.

Services: WCs are scarce. Use them when you can, in any café or museum you patronize. Handy pay WCs are near major landmarks. (At St. Mark's Square, it's behind the Correr Museum.)

Pigeon Poop: If your head is bombed by a pigeon, resist the initial response to wipe it off immediately—it'll just smear into your hair. Wait until it dries, and it should flake off cleanly. But if the poop splatters on your clothes, wipe it off immediately to avoid a stain.

Be Prepared to Splurge: Venice is expensive for residents as well as tourists, as everything must be shipped in and hand-trucked to its destination. I find that the best way to enjoy Venice is just to succumb to its charms and blow a little money.

GETTING AROUND VENICE

On Foot

Venice is delightfully car-free, making pedestrians suddenly feel big, important, and liberated.

The city's "streets" are narrow pedestrian walkways connecting its docks, squares, bridges, and courtyards. To navigate, look for signs on street corners pointing you to (*per*) the nearest major landmark: San Marco, Rialto, Accademia, Ferrovia, or Piazzale Roma.

Some helpful street lingo: *Campo* means square, *calle* is a street, *fondamenta* is an embankment along a canal, *rio* is a small canal, *sotoportego* is a covered passageway, and *ponte* is a bridge.

If you're a map reader, invest in a good one (around €5), or use a smartphone app.

Dare to turn off the posted routes and make your own discoveries. Don't worry about getting lost. Keep reminding yourself, "I'm on an island, and I can't get off." When it comes time to find your way, just follow the signs or simply ask a local, *"Dov'è San Marco?"*

By Vaporetto

These motorized bus-boats run by the public transit system (ACTV) work like city buses except that they never get a flat, the stops are docks, and if you get off between stops, you might drown. For schedules and general information about the vaporettos, see www.veneziaunica.com or www.actv.it.

Tickets and Passes: A single-ride ticket (€7.50 for most trips) is good for 75 minutes in one direction, with unlimited stops and transfers during that time. Or you can buy a pass: €20/24 hours, €30/48 hours, €40/72 hours, or €60/7-day pass. A pass can pay for itself in a hurry, so think through your Venice itinerary before you pay for your first vaporetto trip. On the other hand, many tourists just walk and rarely use a boat.

Buy tickets and passes from the automated machines at most stops, from ticket windows (at larger stops), or from VèneziaUnica offices around town. Tickets are electronic, so you can reuse them for your next trip by putting more money on them at the kiosks (avoiding lines). If the ticket booth at your dock is closed, buy from the conductor when you board. Riding without a ticket risks a big fine.

Riding the Vaporetto: It's very much like catching a bus. Before you board, validate your ticket or pass by holding it up to the small white machine on the dock until you hear a pinging sound. To find your boat, follow signs directing you to the right dock. Each departing boat has a route number (e.g., #1) and also the direction it's headed— for example, "#1 per San Marco." Find that dock and wait for your boat to arrive. The system is simple, though some large stops have multiple docks and multiple lines going in various directions.

Grand Canal Lines #1 and #2: For most travelers, only these two vaporetto lines matter. They leave every 10 minutes or so and go up and down the Grand Canal, between the "mouth" of the fish at one end and San Marco at the other. Line #1 is the slow boat, taking 45 minutes and making every stop along the way. Line #2 takes 25 minutes, making only select stops, including the Tronchetto parking lot, Piazzale Roma, Ferrovia (train station), Rialto Bridge, Accademia Bridge, San Marco, and San Zaccaria (east of St. Mark's Square). Avoid rush hour, when boats can be packed: during mornings heading in from Piazzale Roma, and in evenings heading out to Piazzale Roma. Riding at night, you'll enjoy nearly empty boats and views of chandelier-lit palace interiors.

Handy Vaporetti from San Zaccaria: About 150 yards east of St. Mark's Square are the four San Zaccaria docks, where several helpful boats depart:

• Line #1 goes up the Grand Canal. In the other direction it goes east to Arsenale, Giardini (the Biennale site), and the Lido.

- Line #2 goes up the Grand Canal. In the other direction, it zips over to San Giorgio Maggiore (see page 130).

- Lines #4.1 and #7 both go to Murano in 45 and 25 minutes, respectively.

- Lines #5.1 and #5.2 make a circular loop around the island—perfect if you just like riding boats.

- The Alilaguna airport shuttle to and from the airport stops here.

By Traghetto

These gondola-like, oar-powered boats shuttle locals and in-the-know tourists across the Grand Canal. (Find the stops on the color map at the front of this book.) Just step in, hand the gondolier €2, and enjoy the short ride—standing or sitting. Note that some *traghetti* are seasonal, some stop running as early as 12:30, and all stop by 18:00.

By Water Taxi

Venetian taxis, like speedboat limos, hang out at busy points along the Grand Canal. Prices are regulated: €15 for pick-up, then €2 per minute (plus other supplements). Despite regulation, prices can be soft; negotiate and settle on the price before stepping in. For travelers with lots of luggage, or small groups who can split the cost, taxi-boat rides can be a time-saving convenience. For a little more than €100 an hour, you can have a private, unguided taxi-boat tour. It's pricey, but skipping across the lagoon in a classic wooden motorboat is a cool indulgence. You may find more competitive rates if you prebook through the Consorzio Motoscafi water-taxi association (tel. 041-522-2303, www.motoscafivenezia.it).

STAYING CONNECTED

You can bring your own mobile device (phone, tablet, laptop) and follow my budget tips, buy a European SIM card for your phone, or just use European landlines (in your hotel room) and computers (there's usually one in your hotel lobby). These three options are described in full at www.ricksteves.com/phoning.

Useful Contacts

English-Speaking Police Help: Tel. 112
Ambulance: Tel. 118
US Embassy (in Rome): 24-hour emergency line-tel. 06-46741, nonemergency-tel. 06-4674-2420, by appointment only, http://it.usembassy.gov
US Consulate (in Milan): Tel. 02-290-351, http://it.usembassy.gov/embassy-consulates
Canadian Embassy (in Rome): Tel. 06-854-442-911, www.italy.gc.ca

Making Calls

To call Italy from a US or Canada phone: Dial 011 (international access code), 39 (Italy's country code), and the phone number.

To call Italy from a European phone: Dial 00, then 39 followed by the phone number.

To make calls within Italy: If you're dialing from an Italian mobile phone or landline to another simply dial the phone number, including the initial 0 if there is one.

To call from Italy to another country: Dial 00, the country code, and then the number.

Initial zero: Drop the initial zero from international phone numbers—except when calling Italy.

Mobile Tip: Pressing the + sign auto-selects the correct international access code.

Budget Tips for Using Your Mobile Device in Europe

Use free Wi-Fi whenever possible. Unless you have an unlimited-data plan, save most of your online tasks for Wi-Fi. Many hotels and cafés have Wi-Fi for guests.

Sign up for an international plan. Most providers offer a global plan that cuts the cost of calls and texts, and gives you a block of data. Your normal plan may already include international coverage.

Minimize the use of your cellular network. If you can't find Wi-Fi, you can roam on your cellular network. When you're done, avoid further charges by disabling "cellular data" or roaming in your settings. Save bandwidth-gobbling tasks (Skyping, downloading apps, streaming) for when you're on Wi-Fi.

Use calling/messaging apps for cheaper calls and texts. Some apps (Skype, Viber, FaceTime, Google+ Hangouts) let you call or text for free or cheap when you're on Wi-Fi.

Buy a European SIM card. This option helps you get faster data connections and make voice calls at cheap local rates. Buy a basic phone in Europe (about $40 from a phone shop) or bring an "unlocked" US phone from home. In Italy, tourists should buy SIM cards at mobile-phone shops. You'll be required to register the SIM card with your passport. Once you insert a European SIM, you'll have a European phone number. If you travel to other countries in the European Union, there may be extra roaming fees.

Stick to landlines. If it's inexpensive to make calls from your hotel-room phone (ask at the desk for rates before you dial), you can make your calls even cheaper by using an international phone card (sold at many newsstands, street kiosks, tobacco shops, and train stations).

SIGHTSEEING TIPS

Crowd Control: The city—especially the area from St. Mark's Square to Rialto—is inundated with cruise-ship crowds and day-trippers daily from 10:00 to 16:00, especially on weekends. Sights are most crowded around 11:00-12:00. Visit the St. Mark's Square area early or late, and do your midday sightseeing elsewhere. At St. Mark's Basilica, avoid the line by checking a bag (see page 44) or reserving a time online, and avoid crowds inside by visiting near opening or closing times. At the Doge's Palace, skip the line by buying your combo-ticket (or a Museum Pass) at the uncrowded Correr Museum (see page 66). At the Campanile and Accademia, visit early or late.

Hours: Most sights keep stable hours, but you can easily confirm the latest at a TI, or tel. 041-529-8711, or at www.turismovenezia.it.

Venice Early and Late: Sights that open before 10:00 include the Accademia, Doge's Palace, Campanile, and many churches. Sights that stay open later than 18:00 (at least on some days) include the Accademia, Campanile, Correr Museum, and the Doge's Palace.

What to Expect: Important sights have metal detectors or conduct bag searches that will slow your entry. Some don't allow large bags. Photos and videos are normally allowed, but flashes or tripods usually are not. Many sights stop admitting people 30-60 minutes before closing time, and guards start shooing people out, so don't save the best for last.

Dress Code at Churches: St. Mark's Basilica allows no bare shoulders or knees. Other churches encourage modest dress but don't enforce it.

Discounts: Youth and senior discounts are available to Americans and other non-EU citizens (bring ID) at a few museums, including the Doge's Palace, Correr Museum, and Ca' Rezzonico. Other museums generally do not offer discounts, but you can always ask. Italian state-run museums, such as the Accademia, offer free admission on some Sundays in the off-season.

Pace Yourself: Venice's endless pavement, crowds, and tight spaces are hard on tourists. Schedule cool breaks to refresh. If you must, pay for a drink in a café for the privilege of sitting.

Rick Steves Audio Europe: My free smartphone app makes it easy to download my audio tours of top attractions, plus hours of travel interviews, all organized into destination-specific playlists. I've produced free, self-guided audio tours of the Grand Canal, St. Mark's Square, St. Mark's Basilica, and the Frari Church. You can download Rick Steves Audio Europe via Apple's App Store, Google Play, or the Amazon Appstore. For more information, see www.ricksteves.com/audioeurope.

Sightseeing Passes for Venice

Venice offers an array of passes for sightseeing and transit. None of the options are a must-have, but for most people, the **Museum Pass** (€24) can save some money and time in line. It covers the Doge's Palace/ Correr Museum, Ca' Rezzonico, Palazzo Mocenigo Costume Museum, Ca' Pesaro, and several lesser museums. If you see the Doge's Palace/ Correr Museum, and even just one other museum, this pass is the best value. Buy the Museum Pass at any participating museum. Families get a price break on multiple passes—ask.

Venice's other passes—e.g., the Chorus Pass (covering churches, €12) and the Venice Card (also called a "city pass," churches plus museums, €40)—are unlikely to pay for themselves. Note that a few major sights are not included in any pass: Accademia, Peggy Guggenheim

Collection, Scuola San Rocco, Campanile, and the three museums within St. Mark's Basilica.

THEFT AND EMERGENCIES

Theft: While violent crime is rare in Venice, thieves—mainly well-dressed pickpockets—thrive in crowds. Be alert to the possibility of theft, even when you're absorbed in the wonder and newness of Venice. Be on guard whenever crowds press together, while you're preoccupied at ticket windows, and anywhere around major sights. Be especially alert inside St. Mark's Basilica, near the Accademia or Rialto bridges (especially if you're preoccupied with snapping photos), and on crowded vaporettos (boarding and leaving, in particular). Assume that any commotion nearby is a distraction by a team of thieves. On the plus side, the dark, late-night streets of Venice are generally safe.

I keep my valuables—passport, credit cards, crucial documents, and large amounts of cash—in a money belt that I tuck under my beltline.

Dial 112 for English-speaking police help. A handy *polizia* station is on the right side of St. Mark's Square (near Caffè Florian). If you feel ripped off by any gondoliers, shop owners, hotels, or restaurants, submit your complaint in writing to the Venice TI (complaint.apt@turismovenezia.it). To replace a passport, contact an embassy or consulate (for contact info, see page 191). File a police report without delay; it's required to submit an insurance claim for lost or stolen rail passes or travel gear, and can help with replacing your passport or credit and debit cards. For more information, see www.ricksteves.com/help.

Medical Help: Dial 112 for English-speaking police/medical emergencies, or 118 for an ambulance. If you get sick, do as the Italians do and go to a pharmacy, where qualified technicians routinely diagnose and prescribe. Or ask at your hotel for help—they'll know the nearest medical and emergency services. Venice's hospital ("Ospedale"), officially called Santi Giovanni e Paolo Hospital, is a 10-minute walk east of Rialto or 10 minutes north of San Marco, on Fondamenta dei Mendicanti.

ACTIVITIES

Shopping

Venice is a great shopping town, known for its sense of style since it first dealt in exotic imports from the East. It offers the full range, from glitzy high-fashion boutiques to street vendors selling wacky T-shirts. Remember, anything not made locally is brought in by boat—and therefore more expensive than elsewhere in Italy. But in this city of aristocrats and luxury goods, shopping has a charm that makes paying too much strangely enjoyable.

Shops are typically open Monday to Saturday 9:00-19:30, and more stores are open on Sunday here than in the rest of the country. If you're buying a substantial amount from nearly any shop, bargain—it's accepted and almost expected. To get the best price, offer to pay cash.

Sizes: European clothing sizes are different from the US. For example, a woman's size 10 dress (US) is a European size 40, and a size 8 shoe (US) is a European size 38-39.

Getting a VAT Refund: If you spend more than €155 on goods at a single store, you may be eligible to get a refund of the 22 percent Value-Added Tax (VAT). You'll need to ask the merchant to fill out the necessary refund document, then process your refund through a service such as Global Blue or Premier Tax Free, with offices at major airports. For more details, see www.ricksteves.com/vat.

Customs for American Shoppers: You are allowed to take home $800 worth of items per person duty-free, once every 31 days. You can also bring home one liter of alcohol duty-free. As for food, you can take home many processed and packaged foods (e.g., vacuum-packed cheeses, chocolate, mustard). Fresh produce and most meats are not allowed. Any liquid-containing foods must be packed (carefully) in checked luggage. To check customs rules and duty rates, visit http://help.cbp.gov.

Normal Goods: For ordinary clothing and housewares, the best all-purpose department store is the Coin store on the east side of the Rialto Bridge (from the bridge, head north toward Ferrovia).

Cheap Knock-Offs: Along Venice's many shopping streets, fly-by-night street vendors sell fake designer-label handbags at great prices. (Offer even less.) But buyer beware: It's illegal, and if you're caught purchasing fakes, even you could get hit with a fine. Whenever police saunter by, the vendors gather up and scurry away.

Shopping Walk: To get an overview of Venetian shopping, start in St. Mark's Square, with its pricey smorgasbord of Venetian goods. Exit under the Clock Tower onto the Mercerie, lined with fancy window displays. Cross Rialto Bridge (lots of tempting shops) to the west side and walk through a long block of street vendors. Turn left onto the Ruga Vechia San Giovanni, heading into in a neighborhood with plenty of inviting shops, but fewer crowds and better prices.

Souvenir Ideas

Popular souvenirs are Murano glass, Burano lace, Carnevale masks, art reproductions (posters, postcards, and books), original art (browse the galleries near the Peggy Guggenheim Collection), traditional stationery (pens and marbled paper), high-fashion clothing (silk ties and scarves), and plenty of goofy knickknacks—Titian mousepads, gondolier T-shirts, or little plastic gondola condom holders.

Venetian Glass: Since medieval times, Venetian glassmakers have created vases, wine glasses, jewelry, sculptures, and more. If you buy, shops will ship it home for you, though the shipping can cost as much as the purchase. Make sure they guarantee to replace any items that arrive broken. For a less-fragile, packable souvenir, consider glass-bead jewelry.

To watch a quick glassblowing demonstration, try Galleria San Marco, just off St. Mark's Square at #181a (on Calle del Cappello Nero). Every few minutes they do a demo, followed by a soft-sell sales pitch. Though it's designed for tour groups, they let individual travelers flashing this book sneak in. Enter the shop and climb the stairs (daily 8:30-17:00, tel. 041-271-8671, info@galleriasanmarco.it).

If you're serious about glass, visit the island of Murano, with its glass museum and many shops (see page 148). You'll find greater variety on Murano, but prices are about the same as in Venice. Beware glass products made in China—genuine Venetian glass comes with the Murano seal.

Masks: In the 1700s, when Venice was Europe's party town, masks were popular to preserve the anonymity of visiting nobles doing things forbidden back home. The tradition continues today at Carnevale (Mardi Gras). Masks are papier-mâché: You make a mold of clay, drape layers of paper and glue atop the mold, let it dry, remove it, and paint it. There are shops all over town. Near the Church of San Zaccaria (just north, on Fondamente de l'Osmarin) try Ca' del Sol and Atelier Marega (and also visit the wood-carving shop next door). Near the Frari Church is Tragicomica (see page 114).

Entertainment and Nightlife

You must experience Venice after dark. The city is quiet at night, as the masses of day-trippers return to their cruise ships and cheap mainland hotels. When the sun goes down, a cool breeze blows in from the lagoon, the lanterns come on, the peeling plaster glows in the moonlight, and Venice resumes its position as Europe's most romantic city.

For me, the best evening entertainment is simply wandering. (Even Venice's dark and distant back lanes are considered safe after nightfall.) Enjoy the orchestras on St. Mark's Square. Pop into small bars for an appetizer and a drink. Lick gelato.

Though Venice comes alive after dark, it does not party into the wee hours. By 22:00, restaurants are winding down; by 23:00, many bars are closing; and by midnight, the city is shut tight.

Get the latest on Venice's busy schedule of events at the TI (www.turismovenezia.it) or the magazine *Un Ospite di Venezia* (free at fancy hotels, or check www.unospitedivenezia.it/en).

St. Mark's Square at Night: For tourists, St. Mark's Square is the highlight, with lantern light and live music echoing from the cafés. Every night, enthusiastic musicians play the same songs, creating the same irresistible magic. Listen for free from a distance, or spring for a seat and a drink; it can be €15 and up—money well spent. For more on the cafés and their prices, see page 34.

Live Chamber Music: Venice is a city of the powdered-wig Baroque era, and composer Antonio Vivaldi is a hometown boy. A number of venues offer Vivaldi's *Four Seasons* and other chamber music, in a candlelit historic ambience, for about €25. You'll see posters all over town, and they rarely sell out. Buy tickets at the door, from your hotel (no service charge), or from frilly young Vivaldis hawking concert tickets on street corners. San Vidal Church (north end of Accademia Bridge) has concerts almost nightly, featuring what may be the best group in town, the Interpreti Veneziani orchestra (tel. 041-277-0561, www.interpretiveneziani.com).

Other Performances: Venice's most famous theaters are La Fenice (grand old opera house, box office tel. 041-2424, see page 130),

Teatro Goldoni (mostly Italian live theater), and Teatro Fondamenta Nuove (theater, music, and dance). *Musica a Palazzo* is a unique, intimate evening of opera at a Venetian palace on the Grand Canal (mobile 340-971-7272, www.musicapalazzo.com).

Pubs, Clubs, and Late-Night Scenes: Venice's few *discoteche* are overpriced, exclusive, and not tourist-friendly. But there are a few good places people gather to enjoy the late hours. At the west end of Rialto Bridge, there's a cluster of youthful, trendy bars near the Rialto Market (see the "Bancogiro Stretch" on page 165). East of Rialto Bridge is the local-oriented Devil's Forest Pub (San Marco 5185, on Calle Stagneri, www.devilsforestpub.com). The Dorsoduro neighborhood, south of Accademia Bridge, has two late-night zones: Zattere, on the southern bank, and student-friendly Campo Santa Margarita. Near Campo Santa Margarita, the Venice Jazz Club has live music at 21:00 (€20, no music Thu and Sun, near Ponte dei Pugni, Dorsoduro 3102, tel. 041-523-2056, www.venicejazzclub.com).

Gondolas

For centuries, gondolas ferried aristocrats through Venice's watery "streets." Today, they're strictly for tourists. The long, sleek, flat-bottomed boats are perfect for navigating the shallow lagoon, and the oarsman stands up to see. The gondola curves a bit on the oar side so that a thrust sends the gondola in a straight line. Each boat has unique upholstery, trim, and detailing, such as the squiggly shaped, carved-wood oarlock (*fórcola*) and metal "hood ornament" (*ferro*). Today, there are about 400 licensed gondoliers. And do the gondoliers sing, as the popular image has it? My mom asked our gondolier that very question, and he replied, "Madame, there are the lovers and there are the singers. I do not sing."

Riding a Gondola: Taking a gondola ride is simple but expensive. While this is a rip-off for some, it's a traditional must for romantics.

The price starts at €80 per boat—that is, €40 per person for a couple—for a 35-minute ride during the day. You can divide the cost—and the romance—among up to six people per boat, but only two get the love seat. Prices jump to €100 after 19:00—when it's most romantic and relaxing. Adding a singer and an accordionist will cost an additional €120. Prices are standard and listed at www.gondolavenezia.it (click on "Using the Gondola," and look under *"charterage"*).

Shop around and choose a gondolier you click with. Striped-shirted gondoliers hang out all over town. Talk to him about the route and how long the ride is. While rates are standard, he may quote a higher price—politely talk him down, or even go lower (prices are soft during the day). Establish the final price, route, duration, and even whether he expects a tip at the end (it's not obligatory). Do all this before you board, and pay only when you're finished. Then relax and enjoy the ride, gliding through Venice with your head on someone's shoulder.

Guided Tours

Many companies offer English-language, two- to three-hour small-group tours of Venice's sights, for around €25-75 a person. Some offer a Rick Steves discount—it's worth asking.

Avventure Bellissime offers several different walks, including St. Mark's Square and a boat tour of the Grand Canal (tel. 041-970-499, www.tours-italy.com, info@tours-italy.com). Artviva's tours include Venice Walk, Grand Canal, Doge's Palace, and a "learn to be a gondolier" tour (www.italy.artviva.com). Michael Broderick's tours are long and intellectually demanding, for serious students of Venice (tel. 041-850-5742, www.venicescapes.org, info@venicescapes.org). Debonair Alessandro Schezzini takes groups on a fun two-hour pub crawl of back lanes and *cicchetti* bars (mobile 335-530-9024, www.schezzini.it, alessandro@schezzini.it).

You could hire your own private guide for around €150 for a two-hour tour. Here are a few: "Walks Inside Venice" (www.walksinside-venice.com, info@walksinsidevenice.com, or call Roberta at mobile 347-253-0560); Elisabetta Morelli (mobile 328-753-5220, bettamo-relli@inwind.it); and "Venice with a Guide" (www.venicewithaguide.com).

RESOURCES FROM RICK STEVES

This Pocket guide is one of dozens of titles in my series of guidebooks on European travel. I also produce a public television series, *Rick Steves' Europe*, and a public radio show, *Travel with Rick Steves*. My website, www.ricksteves.com, offers a wealth of free travel resources, including videos and podcasts of my shows, audio tours of Europe's great sights, travel forums, guidebook updates, and information on European rail passes—plus an online travel store and specifics on our tours of Europe. My audio tours and other audio content are available for free through my ⌒ Rick Steves Audio Europe app, an extensive online library organized into handy geographic playlists. If you have feedback on this book, please fill out the survey at www.ricksteves. com/feedback. It helps us and fellow travelers.

Italian Survival Phrases

English	Italian	Pronunciation
Good day.	Buon giorno.	bwohn JOR-noh
Do you speak English?	Parla inglese?	PAR-lah een-GLAY-zay
Yes. / No.	Sì. / No.	see / noh
I (don't) understand.	(Non) capisco.	(nohn) kah-PEES-koh
Please.	Per favore.	pehr fah-VOH-ray
Thank you.	Grazie.	GRAHT-seeay
You're welcome.	Prego.	PRAY-go
I'm sorry.	Mi dispiace.	mee dee-speeAH-chay
Excuse me.	Mi scusi.	mee SKOO-zee
(No) problem.	(Non) c'è un problema.	(nohn) cheh oon proh-BLAY-mah
Good.	Va bene.	vah BEHN-ay
Goodbye.	Arrivederci.	ah-ree-vay-DEHR-chee
one / two	uno / due	OO-noh / DOO-ay
three / four	tre / quattro	tray / KWAH-troh
five / six	cinque / sei	CHEENG-kway / SEHee
seven / eight	sette / otto	SEHT-tay / OT-toh
nine / ten	nove / dieci	NOV-ay / deeAY-chee
How much is it?	Quanto costa?	KWAHN-toh KOS-tah
Write it?	Me lo scrive?	may loh SKREE-vay
Is it free?	È gratis?	eh GRAH-tees
Is it included?	È incluso?	eh een-KLOO-zoh
Where can I buy / find...?	Dove posso comprare / trovare...?	DOH-vay POS-soh kohm-PRAH-ray / troh-VAH-ray
I'd like / We'd like...	Vorrei / Vorremmo...	vor-REHee / vor-RAY-moh
...a room.	...una camera.	OO-nah KAH-meh-rah
...a ticket to ___.	...un biglietto per ___.	oon beel-YEHT-toh pehr
Is it possible?	È possibile?	eh poh-SEE-bee-lay
Where is...?	Dov'è...?	DOH-veh
...the train station	...la stazione	lah staht-seeOH-nay
...the bus station	...la stazione degli autobus	lah staht-seeOH-nay DAYL-yee OW-toh-boos
...tourist information	...informazioni per turisti	een-for-maht-seeOH-nee pehr too-REE-stee
...the toilet	...la toilette	lah twah-LEHT-tay
men	uomini, signori	WOH-mee-nee, seen-YOH-ree
women	donne, signore	DON-nay, seen-YOH-ray
left / right	sinistra / destra	see-NEE-strah / DEHS-trah
straight	sempre diritto	SEHM-pray dee-REE-toh
When do you open / close?	A che ora aprite / chiudete?	ah kay OH-rah ah-PREE-tay / keeoo-DAY-tay
At what time?	A che ora?	ah kay OH-rah
Just a moment.	Un momento.	oon moh-MAYN-toh
now / soon / later	adesso / presto / tardi	ah-DEHS-soh / PREHS-toh / TAR-dee
today / tomorrow	oggi / domani	OH-jee / doh-MAH-nee

In the Restaurant

English	Italian	Pronunciation
I'd like...	Vorrei...	vor-REHee
We'd like...	Vorremmo...	vor-RAY-moh
...to reserve...	...prenotare...	pray-noh-TAH-ray
...a table for one / two.	...un tavolo per uno / due.	oon TAH-voh-loh pehr OO-noh / DOO-ay
Non-smoking.	Non fumare.	nohn foo-MAH-ray
Is this seat free?	È libero questo posto?	eh LEE-bay-roh KWEHS-toh POH-stoh
The menu (in English), please.	Il menù (in inglese), per favore.	eel may-NOO (een een-GLAY-zay) pehr fah-VOH-ray
service (not) included	servizio (non) incluso	sehr-VEET-seeoh (nohn) een-KLOO-zoh
cover charge	pane e coperto	PAH-nay ay koh-PEHR-toh
to go	da portar via	dah POR-tar VEE-ah
with / without	con / senza	kohn / SEHN-sah
and / or	e / o	ay / oh
menu (of the day)	menù (del giorno)	may-NOO (dayl JOR-noh)
specialty of the house	specialità della casa	spay-chah-lee-TAH DEHL-lah KAH-zah
first course (pasta, soup)	primo piatto	PREE-moh peeAH-toh
main course (meat, fish)	secondo piatto	say-KOHN-doh peeAH-toh
side dishes	contorni	kohn-TOR-nee
bread	pane	PAH-nay
cheese	formaggio	for-MAH-joh
sandwich	panino	pah-NEE-noh
soup	minestra, zuppa	mee-NEHS-trah, TSOO-pah
salad	insalata	een-sah-LAH-tah
dessert	dolci	DOHL-chee
tap water	acqua del rubinetto	AH-kwah dayl roo-bee-NAY-toh
mineral water	acqua minerale	AH-kwah mee-nay-RAH-lay
milk	latte	LAH-tay
(orange) juice	succo (d'arancia)	SOO-koh (dah-RAHN-chah)
coffee / tea	caffè / tè	kah-FEH / teh
wine	vino	VEE-noh
red / white	rosso / bianco	ROH-soh / beeAHN-koh
glass / bottle	bicchiere / bottiglia	bee-keeAY-ray / boh-TEEL-yah
beer	birra	BEE-rah
Cheers!	Cin cin!	cheen cheen
More. / Another.	Ancora un po.' / Un altro.	ahn-KOH-rah oon poh / oon AHL-troh
The same.	Lo stesso.	loh STEHS-soh
The bill, please.	Il conto, per favore.	eel KOHN-toh pehr fah-VOH-ray
tip	mancia	MAHN-chah
Delicious!	Delizioso!	day-leet-seeOH-zoh

For more user-friendly Italian phrases, check out *Rick Steves' Italian Phrase Book & Dictionary* or *Rick Steves' French, Italian, and German Phrase Book*.

INDEX

Start your trip at

Our website enhances this book and turns

Explore Europe

At ricksteves.com you can browse through thousands of articles, videos, photos and radio interviews, plus find a wealth of money-saving travel tips for planning your dream trip. And with our mobile-friendly website, you can easily access all this great travel information anywhere you go.

TV Shows

Preview the places you'll visit by watching entire half-hour episodes of Rick Steves' Europe (choose from all 100 shows) on-demand, for free.

ricksteves.com

your travel dreams into affordable reality

Radio Interviews

Enjoy ready access to Rick's vast library of radio interviews covering

travel tips and cultural insights that relate specifically to your Europe travel plans.

Travel Forums

Learn, ask, share! Our online community of savvy travelers is a great resource for first-time travelers to Europe, as well as seasoned pros. You'll find forums on each country, plus travel tips and restaurant/hotel reviews. You can even ask one of our well-traveled staff to chime in with an opinion.

Travel News

Subscribe to our free Travel News e-newsletter, and get monthly updates from Rick on what's happening in Europe.

Audio Europe™

Rick's Free Travel App

Get your FREE Rick Steves Audio Europe™ app to enjoy...

- Dozens of self-guided tours of Europe's top museums, sights and historic walks
- Hundreds of tracks filled with cultural insights and sightseeing tips from Rick's radio interviews
- All organized into handy geographic playlists
- For Apple and Android

With Rick whispering in your ear, Europe gets even better.

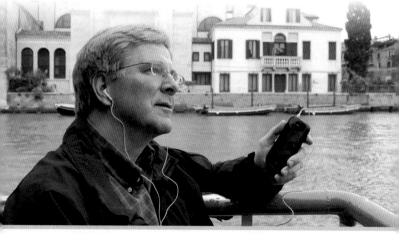

Find out more at ricksteves.com

Pack Light and Right

Gear up for your next adventure at ricksteves.com

Light Luggage

Pack light and right with Rick Steves' affordable, custom-designed rolling carry-on bags, backpacks, day packs and shoulder bags.

Accessories

From packing cubes to moneybelts and beyond, Rick has personally selected the travel goodies that will help your trip go smoother.

Shop at ricksteves.com

Rick Steves has

Experience maximum Europe

Save time and energy

This guidebook is your independent-travel toolkit. But for all it delivers, it's still up to you to devote the time and energy it takes to manage the preparation and logistics that are essential for a happy trip. If that's a hassle, there's a solution.

Rick Steves Tours

A Rick Steves tour takes you to Europe's most interesting places with great guides and small groups

great tours, too!

with minimum stress

of 28 or less. We follow Rick's favorite itineraries, ride in comfy buses, stay in family-run hotels, and bring you intimately close to the Europe you've traveled so far to see. Most importantly, we take away the logistical headaches so you can focus on the fun.

Join the fun

This year we'll take thousands of free-spirited travelers—nearly half of them repeat customers—along with us on four dozen different itineraries, from Ireland to Italy to Istanbul. Is a Rick Steves tour the right fit for your travel dreams? Find out at ricksteves.com, where you can also request Rick's latest tour catalog.

Europe is best experienced with happy travel partners. We hope you can join us.

See our itineraries at ricksteves.com

A Guide for Every Trip

BEST OF GUIDES
Full-color guides in an easy-to-scan format, focusing on top sights and experiences in popular destinations

Best of England
Best of Europe
Best of France
Best of Germany

Best of Ireland
Best of Italy
Best of Scotland
Best of Spain

COMPREHENSIVE GUIDES
City, country, and regional guides printed on Bible-thin paper. Packed with detailed coverage for a multi-week trip exploring iconic sights and more

Amsterdam &
   the Netherlands
Barcelona
Belgium: Bruges, Brussels,
   Antwerp & Ghent
Berlin
Budapest
Croatia & Slovenia
Eastern Europe
England
Florence & Tuscany
France
Germany
Great Britain
Greece: Athens &
   the Peloponnese
Iceland

Ireland
Istanbul
Italy
London
Paris
Portugal
Prague & the Czech Republic
Provence & the French
   Riviera
Rome
Scandinavia
Scotland
Sicily
Spain
Switzerland
Venice
Vienna, Salzburg & Tirol

Rick Steves books are available from your favorite bookseller.
Many guides are available as ebooks.

POCKET GUIDES
Compact guides for shorter city trips

Amsterdam	Italy's Cinque Terre	Prague
Athens	London	Rome
Barcelona	Munich & Salzburg	Venice
Florence	Paris	Vienna

SNAPSHOT GUIDES
Focused single-destination coverage

Basque Country: Spain & France
Copenhagen & the Best of Denmark
Dublin
Dubrovnik
Edinburgh
Hill Towns of Central Italy
Krakow, Warsaw & Gdansk
Lisbon
Loire Valley
Madrid & Toledo
Milan & the Italian Lakes District
Naples & the Amalfi Coast
Nice & the French Riviera
Normandy
Northern Ireland
Norway
Reykjavík
Rothenburg & the Rhine
Sevilla, Granada & Southern Spain
St. Petersburg, Helsinki & Tallinn
Stockholm

CRUISE PORTS GUIDES
Reference for cruise ports of call

Mediterranean Cruise Ports
Scandinavian & Northern European
  Cruise Ports

TRAVEL SKILLS & CULTURE
Greater information and insight

Europe 101: History and Art for
  the Traveler
Europe Through the Back Door:
  the Travel Skills Handbook
European Christmas
European Easter
European Festivals
Postcards from Europe
Travel as a Political Act

PHRASE BOOKS & DICTIONARIES

French
French, Italian & German
German
Italian
Portuguese
Spanish

PLANNING MAPS

Britain, Ireland & London
Europe
France & Paris
Germany, Austria & Switzerland
Iceland
Ireland
Italy
Spain & Portugal

PHOTO CREDITS